How to Preach Apocalyptic

How to Preach Apocalyptic

Ryan Boys

Fontes

How to Preach Apocalyptic

Copyright © 2024 by Ryan Boys

ISBN-13: 978-1-948048-95-8 (paperback)
ISBN-13: 978-1-948048-96-5 (epub)

All rights reserved. No part of this publication may be reproduced, stored in a retrieval system, or transmitted in any form or by any means—electronic, mechanical, photocopy, recording, or any other—except for brief quotations in printed reviews, without the prior permission of the publisher.

Scripture quotations marked CSB have been taken from the Christian Standard Bible®, Copyright © 2017 by Holman Bible Publishers. Used by permission. Christian Standard Bible® and CSB® are federally registered trademarks of Holman Bible Publishers.

Typeset by Monolateral™ in Minion 3 and Museo Sans.

FONTES PRESS
DALLAS, TX
www.fontespress.com

For my beloved Lindsay, who has endured for many years my attempts to preach the apocalyptic literature of the Bible.

Contents

Series Introduction.. xvii

Preface xix

Introduction... 1
    What Is Apocalyptic Literature? 3
    Literary Features of Apocalyptic Literature 6
    The Game Plan 7
    For Further Study.. 10
    Talk about It 10
    Dig Deeper... 10
    Practice 10

1. Apocalyptic as Narrative: Every Vision is a Story 11
    Interpretive Insights...................................... 12
        Find the Story: Identifying Flat Narrative Plots......... 12
        Find the Story: Identifying Climactic Narrative Plots... 13
        Enjoy the View: Exposition Embedded in Vision Reports ... 16
    Homiletical Strategy 1: Tell the Story..................... 18
        Set the Stage 18
        Rising Action 19
        Climax and Solution 21
        Summary of Homiletical Strategy 1 22
    Homiletical Strategy 2: Divide the Text Appropriately .. 22
        Getting Used to Apocalyptic Vision Narratives 23
        Induction vs. Deduction 26
        Handling Long Passages 27
        A Sermon Series on Apocalyptic Literature 27
        Summary of Homiletical Strategy 2 29
    For Further Study.. 29
    Talk about It 29
    Dig Deeper... 30
    Practice 30

2. **Apocalyptic Characterization: The Cast of Participants in the Vision** 31
    Interpretive Insights 32
        A Special Kind of Protagonist 32
        The Heavenly Mediator 33
        There Is Only One Hero 35
        Supporting Cast 35
        Who Is the Bad Guy? 37
    Homiletical Strategy 3: Invite Hearers to Journey
    with the Prophet 38
        Connect the Audience with the Prophet 39
        Instill Confidence in God 40
        Emphasize Shocking Characters 42
        Call the Audience to Perseverance 42
        Confront with Care 43
        Summary of Homiletical Strategy 3 44
    For Further Study 44
    Talk about It 45
    Dig Deeper 45
    Practice 45

3. **Aural Effects of Apocalyptic: The Sound of the Vision** 47
    Interpretive Insights 48
        Alliteration 49
        Assonance 49
        Rhyme 50
        Onomatopoeia 51
        Wordplay 51
    Homiletical Strategy 4: Echo the Aural Effect 52
        Use an Equivalent to Alliteration 53
        Recreate or Explain Assonance 54
        Reproduce the Effect of Rhyme 56
        Recreate the Effect of Onomatopoeia 56
        Explain the Aural Effect of Wordplay 58
        Non-Aural Techniques 59
        Summary of Homiletical Strategy 4 59
    For Further Study 60

- Talk about It 60
- Dig Deeper 60
- Practice 60

4. **APOCALYPTIC FIGURATIVE LANGUAGE: SIGNS, SYMBOLS, AND NUMBERS** 61
   - Interpretive Insights 62
     - *The Symbolic Nature of Visions: Signs and Referents* .. 62
     - *Specific Signs in Apocalyptic* 65
     - *People* 65
     - *Animals* 66
     - *Natural Elements* 68
     - *Props* 69
     - *Angelic Actions* 71
     - *Spiritually Significant Numbers* 72
   - Homiletical Strategy 5: Paint the Picture 74
     - *Personalize a Generic Sign* 75
     - *Use Vivid Language and Imagery* 76
     - *Use Analogies* 76
     - *Be Clear with Numbers* 77
     - *Summary of Homiletical Strategy 5* 78
   - Homiletical Strategy 6: Follow the Vision Interpreter ... 79
     - *Explain the Nature of Signs and Symbols* 79
     - *Be Clear on What Is Clear* 80
     - *Focus on the Why* 82
     - *Avoid Overselling Uncertain Identifications of Signs and Symbols* 83
     - *Deal with Controversial, Unfamiliar, or Unusual Signs* 85
     - *Refuse to Generalize the Message* 86
     - *Summary of Homiletical Strategy 6* 87
   - For Further Study 88
   - Talk about It 88
   - Dig Deeper 88
   - Practice 89

5. APOCALYPTIC TRANSCENDENT PERSPECTIVE: GOOD, EVIL, AND REVOLUTIONARY THINKING..........................91
   - Interpretive Insights..91
     - *A Resolution to the Problem of Evil*....................92
     - *Visions of Victory*.......................................93
     - *Visions of the Judgment of the Wicked*..................95
   - Homiletical Strategy 7: Offer Hope......................96
     - *Honestly Appraise Evil and Suffering*..................96
     - *Give Glimpses of Victory*..............................100
     - *Identify Faulty Views of Victory*......................101
     - *Point to the Just Judge*...............................103
     - *Identify Faulty Views of Justice*......................105
     - *Call for a Revolution*.................................106
     - *Summary of Homiletical Strategy 7*....................107
   - For Further Study..108
   - Talk about It...108
   - Dig Deeper...108
   - Practice..108

6. LITERARY CONTEXT OF APOCALYPTIC VISIONS: VISIONS AS A PART OF THE WHOLE..................................111
   - Interpretive Insights.....................................111
     - *Implications of Inspiration—How Does Apocalyptic Fit?*..113
     - *Literary Structure Matters*............................114
   - Homiletical Strategy 8: Connect the Contextual Dots...114
     - *Unpack the Immediate Context of the Book*............115
     - *Disclose the Message of the Book*.....................116
     - *Show How the Vision Contributes to the Message of the Book*...117
     - *Summary of Homiletical Strategy 8*....................121
   - Homiletical Strategy 9: Preach the Gospel..............121
     - *Does this Vision Prophesy about the Messiah?*........124
     - *Does this Vision Reveal the Need for Redemption?*....126
     - *Does this Vision Show God's Judgment or Salvation?*..127
     - *Does This Vision Point to an Aspect of Redemption?*..132
     - *Summary of Homiletical Strategy 9*....................134
   - Homiletical Strategy 10: Reveal the Eschatology........134
     - *Preach with Humility*..................................135

  Aim for Theological Clarity 137
  Stay Grounded in the Text 137
  Summary of Homiletical Strategy 10 139
 For Further Study.. 139
 Talk about It 140
 Dig Deeper... 140
 Practice 140

7. RHETORICAL EFFECTS OF APOCALYPTIC VISIONS: WHAT'S THE POINT? 141
 Interpretive Insights 142
  Apocalyptic Gets the Attention of the Audience........ 143
  Apocalyptic Transforms Perspective 144
  Apocalyptic Comforts the Suffering.................... 145
  Apocalyptic Encourages Perseverance 145
  Apocalyptic Fosters Worship 146
  Apocalyptic Calls for Repentance 148
 Homiletical Strategy 11: Aim for a Similar Rhetorical Effect... 148
  Shock and Awe 149
  Transform Perspectives................................151
  Provide Comfort in Trials............................. 152
  Motivate Perseverance 153
  Foster Worship.. 154
  Call to Repentance 156
  Summary of Homiletical Strategy 11 157
 Homiletical Strategy 12: Plan Worship Services with Purpose..157
  Tone of the Sermon................................... 158
  The Sermon as It Relates to Other Components of the Worship Service 159
  Summary of Homiletical Strategy 12 162
 For Further Study.. 162
 Talk about It 163
 Dig Deeper... 163
 Practice 163

Conclusion 165

Appendix 1: A Philosophy of Preaching 169
   What I Value in Preaching 169
     (1) Rooted in Exposition 169
     (2) Crafted in Light of the Genre 170
     (3) Informed by Biblical Theology 171
     (4) Saturated with Application 171
     (5) Marked by Clarity 171
     (6) Anchored in the Gospel 172
     (7) Aimed at the Affections 172
     (8) Empowered by the Spirit 172

Appendix 2: Sample Sermons on Old Testament
Apocalyptic Visions 175
   "Big Trouble from the Little Horn" (Daniel 8:1–27) 176
     Opening Hook 176
     Setting Up Daniel 8 176
     The Vision of a Ram and Goat 177
     The Interpretation of the Vision 178
     Reaction and Application 180
   "Wardrobe Change" (Zechariah 3:1–10) 182

Appendix 3: Sample Sermons on New Testament
Apocalyptic Visions 189
   "Vengeance and Vindication" (Revelation 19:11–21) 190
   "We Are at War" (Revelation 12:1–17) 199

Appendix 4: Summary of Apocalyptic Hermeneutical
Insights and Homiletic Strategies 207

Scripture Index 209

Series Introduction

The Bible is the best-selling book of all time. There are various reasons for that—it feeds us spiritually; gives us hope; points us to the Triune God; and shows us where we came from and where we are going. There's another reason: the Bible is great literature; just plain great. Captivating narratives, wry proverbs, dark prophecies, catalogues of laws, and practical but theologically deep epistles populate its pages.

However, the literary nature of the Bible creates a problem for preaching. What's a preacher to do with that fact that the Bible is literature? Are we supposed to create sermonic-poems when we preach psalms? Are we supposed to leave our meaning opaque when we preach certain parables? If the text is a story must the sermon be a story? What's a preacher to do?

One thing preachers could do, and have done, is to ignore the fact that the Bible is literature. Turn a deaf ear and blind eye to its literary qualities. Feed each text into the homiletical mill and crank out sermon after sermon as uniform as hotdogs. The authors of this series reject that option. Our conviction is that God inspired not only the content of the Bible, but also its forms. Cranking out homiletical hotdogs from quirky parables, awe-inspiring miracle stories, kaleidoscopic visions, and emotive lyric poetry violates authorial intention. Ronald Allen famously quipped: "To change the form of preaching to a form not clearly representative of the text is akin to covering the cathedral at Chartres with vinyl siding."[1]

---

1 Ronald J. Allen, "Shaping Sermons by the Language of the Text," in *Preaching Biblically,* ed. Don M. Wardlaw (Westminster, 1983), 30.

The authors share another conviction: preaching should be interesting. Holding an audience's attention is largely a matter of content—showing how the ancient Word applies to today's needs and interests—but it is also a matter of form. A steady diet of hotdogs is unappetizing.

So, how can preachers be biblical in form as well as content? That question is the impetus of this series called *Preaching Biblical Literature*. In trim and readable volumes, the reader will encounter methods and strategies for preaching the various genres of the Bible. We want to give preachers recipes for sermons that are as varied as the literature in the Bible itself.

Our goal is to provide succinct descriptions of these literary forms with concrete suggestions for preaching in genre-sensitive ways. Each volume is grounded in biblical and literary scholarship and applies those disciplines to homiletics. With plenty of examples in each chapter, as well as sample sermons at the end of each book, our hope is to teach and model how to preach biblical literature biblically. Here's to stamping out hotdogs. Let's get cooking.

Jeffrey D. Arthurs
Kenneth J. Langley

Preface

> *Apocalyptic was the mother of Christian Theology.*[1]
>
> Ernst Käsemann

PREACHING THE APOCALYPTIC LITERATURE of the Bible is hard work. In the family of biblical literary genres apocalyptic literature is like an eccentric uncle. Few would claim to understand him, but he is unforgettable. Apocalyptic literature challenges the preacher with angelic guides taking prophets on visionary journeys complete with wild images that are entirely foreign to our culture. Three points and a poem (despite alliteration!) will not cut it for these dramatic texts.

Preachers are well aware of the exegetical difficulties of biblical apocalyptic literature. It would be ideal for every prospective pastor in seminary to take an elective on each prophetic book of the Bible along with a class on the hermeneutics of apocalyptic literature. Ideal or not, this is not practical. Thus, the brave pastor who chooses to preach on an apocalyptic text faces one of the most exegetically challenging parts of the Bible with limited exposure and a lack of resources. The time investment alone in getting up to speed on issues regarding apocalyptic passages is huge. Add to that the differences between eschatological systems, and it is no wonder many pastors hesitate to preach on these parts of the Bible.

Those who do hack their way through the hermeneutical jungle

---

1 Ernst Käsemann, "The Beginnings of Christian Theology," in *New Testament Quotations for Today* (Fortress, 1969), 102.

of apocalyptic literature may be discouraged to find a homiletical jungle waiting for them on the other side. These passages contain bold visions with striking images. How can you effectively explain fantastic apocalyptic animals in a 35–45 minute sermon to a congregation including soccer moms, accountants, single dads, teenagers, and retirees? Many apocalyptic visions are long. How do you summarize big chunks of unfamiliar text? How do you handle these passages in a longer preaching series? Most importantly, how can you appropriately account for the rhetorical impact of apocalyptic literature?

While difficult, the genre itself is not beyond comprehension. Recent advances in the hermeneutics of apocalyptic literature have paved the way for better sermons.[2] Only a handful of resources on preaching apocalyptic have been published, and they date to the late 1990s.[3] These resources offer a few observations about the genre and include many sample sermons. Unfortunately, none applies recent exegetical advancements in understanding apocalyptic to sermon crafting. Jeffrey Arthurs, C. Marvin Pate, and Richard Taylor offer helpful homiletic suggestions in chapters in their respective works, but they are necessarily limited in scope.[4]

When it comes to preaching apocalyptic the preacher must first *catch the vision*—understand the literary features of the genre. Then we will be prepared to *cast the vision*—craft a sermon that takes into account these features. The goal of this volume is to provide familiarity with the literary features of biblical apocalyptic literature and to offer a vision for how sermons in the shape of Scripture handle those features.

Writing on the topic of apocalyptic literature inevitably includes some interaction with eschatology. I will argue that in the

---

2 E.g., Peter Gentry, *How to Read and Understand the Prophets* (Crossway, 2017); Richard A. Taylor, *Interpreting Apocalyptic Literature* (Kregel Academic, 2016); C. Marvin Pate, *Interpreting Revelation and Other Apocalyptic Literature* (Kregel Academic, 2016).

3 David Jacobsen, *Preaching in the New Creation* (Westminster John Knox, 1999); Larry Paul Jones and Jerry L. Sumney, *Preaching Apocalyptic Texts* (Chalice, 1999); Dorothy Jonaitis, *Unmasking Apocalyptic Texts* (Paulist, 2005).

4 Jeffrey Arthurs, *Preaching with Variety* (Kregel Academic, 2007), 178–199; Pate, *Interpreting Revelation*, 171–220; Taylor, *Interpreting Apocalyptic Literature,* 133–177.

majority of cases different eschatological positions do not radically change the application of an apocalyptic text. I attempt to be clear when differences in theological commitments come into play in interpretation and sermon preparation. I am committed to the principle that the text, not an eschatological system, should drive the content of the sermon. Eschatological discussions may be helpful in a sermon on apocalyptic, but the preacher must be ready to limit such digressions if they detract from the message of the text. Putting my cards on the table, I hold to a progressive covenantal view of the unity of the Bible.[5] I interpret the book of Revelation primarily as a futurist, while seeing valid exegetical contributions from the various other views. I interpret the millennial kingdom in Revelation 20 as future, although I would not insist that the duration need be a literal 1,000 years. One of the primary reasons I find the progressive covenantal approach compelling is because it is based on a hermeneutic that recognizes the role of genre in interpretation. Benjamin Merkle notes how progressive covenantalists believe reducing the question of interpretation to a binary choice between literal or symbolic meaning is misguided. This is because they "do not merely choose one or the other but seek to interpret the Bible according to the author's intention, *which is conveyed in literary forms.*"[6]

Fundamentally, apocalyptic means "revelation."[7] Käsemann was right in that the revealing of God's existence, character, purpose, and plan are the mother of Christian theology. We might add that apocalyptic is also the mother of Christian orthopraxy—what God reveals is meant to foster faith-driven obedience in even the darkest of times. The apocalyptic literature of the Bible was written to strengthen faith in people who had lost their confidence in God and his story. The message of biblical apocalyptic is just as relevant today as it was when it was first written. We need biblical apocalyptic literature.

---

5 See Peter J. Gentry and Stephen J. Wellum, *Kingdom Through Covenant* (Crossway, 2012); Stephen J. Wellum and Brent E. Parker, *Progressive Covenantalism* (B&H Academic, 2016).

6 Benjamin L. Merkle, *Discontinuity to Continuity* (Lexham, 2020), 111, emphasis mine.

7 BDAG, 112, s.v. ἀποκαλύπτω, ἀποκάλυψις.

Introduction

All Scripture is inspired by God and is profitable for teaching, for rebuking, for correcting, for training in righteousness, so that the man of God may be complete, equipped for every good work.

2 Timothy 3:16–17

Preaching the apocalyptic literature of the Bible is a homiletical challenge. This difficult genre of Scripture demands careful attention and thorough preparation. No one *masters* preaching apocalyptic. As British climber George Mallory wrote in 1924 while bravely attempting to be the first to climb Mt. Everest: "We're not exultant; but delighted, joyful; soberly astonished.... Have we vanquished an enemy? Not but ourselves...."[1] Preaching apocalyptic is not easy, but by making use of essential helps and experienced guides, it is a worthy, life-changing endeavor. In the end the preacher is not left arrogant, but "soberly astonished" at the beauty, intensity, and power of this portion of the Word of God.

How to Preach Apocalyptic is based on the conviction that the literary form of a biblical passage should affect the form of a sermon on that passage. This is not a new idea. In his groundbreaking work *Preaching and the Literary Forms of the Bible*, Thomas Long asserted that "the literary form and dynamics of a biblical text can

---

1 George Leigh Mallory, *Climbing Everest: the Complete Writings of George Leigh Mallory* (Gibson Square, 2012), 60.

and should be important factors in the preacher's navigation of the distance between text and sermon."[2] More recently, in *Preaching with Variety* Jeffrey Arthurs observed: "The Bible is a cornucopia of literary forms.... Because God has 'taken the trouble' of communicating with such variety, careful exegetes should sit up and take notice."[3]

In 2 Timothy 3:16 the apostle Paul declares all Scripture to be essential and beneficial for the Christian. The adjective "all" includes the difficult apocalyptic texts of the Bible. He goes on in 2 Timothy 4:2 to command preachers: "Preach the word." The church needs biblical apocalyptic texts and preachers need to proclaim them as the Word of God. Without the preaching of apocalyptic texts, the church is less equipped to walk by faith through severe trials. However, this is a tough genre. The uniqueness of any genre in biblical literature brings specific challenges to the sermon preparation process—challenges in hermeneutics and homiletics. Genres like apocalyptic that are difficult hermeneutically will often be difficult homiletically, yet these more difficult genres are given to the church by God as a blessing, not as appendices. Thus, the hard work of preparing quality sermons on biblical apocalyptic is a needed skill worth cultivating.

How can we allow the unique shape of apocalyptic to shape the sermon? How can we be faithful to these powerful, important, and unusual parts of the Bible? How can we preach the text, and let God do his work through his word? If we want to cast the vision of the apocalyptic literature in the Bible, we have to first catch the vision—understand how the genre works. We need to ask the crucial preliminary question: what is apocalyptic literature? The answer to this question necessarily limits what parts of God's Word we identify as apocalyptic and therefore which passages are relevant to this study. In other words, clearly identifying which parts of the Bible are apocalyptic is key not only to exegesis of apocalyptic texts, but also to crafting sermons on them.

---

2 Thomas Long, *Preaching and the Literary Forms of the Bible* (Fortress, 1989), 11.

3 Jeffrey Arthurs, *Preaching with Variety* (Kregel, 2007), 22.

What Is Apocalyptic Literature?

Genre is all about expectations. When we read, "Once upon a time...," we expect a fictional story, specifically a fairy tale. When we read, "A long time ago in a galaxy far, far away...," we expect a fictional story set in space with a certain shared set of assumptions about a struggle between the Galactic Empire or New Order and a revolutionary minority. We know what a Western is, and we know the difference between a comic strip, an obituary, and a news report. When we identify a genre, it prepares us for what is coming and provides a specific set of guidelines for interpreting what we are reading or watching.

The existence of a genre depends on the identification of a group of texts that share certain literary features. Technically, a literary genre "consists of a group of texts which exhibit a coherent and recurring pattern of features constituted by the interrelated elements of form, content and function."[4] In the nineteenth century biblical scholars began to recognize that a sub-genre existed within prophetic works. As a result, a more precise definition of "apocalyptic literature" began to emerge. Arthurs summarizes this recognition of the genre: "As a term denoting a genre, apocalyptic first appeared in biblical criticism at the beginning of the nineteenth century to refer to visionary eschatological literature, but the genre itself existed from the Babylonian exile (586 B.C.) to the destruction of Jerusalem (A.D. 135)."[5] The birth of a field of study on apocalyptic texts led to the identification of literary features common to these texts.

What, then, is the genre of apocalyptic literature? As it happens, there has been significant disagreement on that question.[6] The term "apocalyptic literature" is often and regrettably used without precision in biblical studies. By "apocalyptic" most people mean "having to do with the end times." Using that broad definition,

---

4 David Aune, "The Apocalypse of John and the Problem of Genre," *Semeia* 36 (1986): 66.

5 Arthurs, *Preaching with Variety*, 179–180.

6 See Richard A. Taylor, *Interpreting Apocalyptic Literature* (Kregel, 2016), 27–30 for a helpful summary of the different approaches.

any biblical passage that speaks of eschatological issues is apocalyptic. Upon closer inspection, apocalyptic texts have a group of genre-defining literary traits.

Studies in apocalyptic and proto-apocalyptic texts from a variety of cultures and times, including biblical literature, have advanced our understanding of the shared literary features of apocalyptic literature. One SBL study group honed a precise definition of apocalyptic literature in 1986 which has been the basis of subsequent refinements.

> "Apocalypse" is a genre of revelatory literature with a narrative framework, in which a revelation is mediated by an otherworldly being to a human recipient, disclosing a transcendent reality which is both temporal insofar as it envisages eschatological salvation, and spatial insofar as it involves another, supernatural world, intended to interpret present, earthly circumstances in light of the super-natural world and of the future, and to influence both the understanding and the behavior of the audience by means of divine authority.[7]

While there is not a consensus on all of the details of what constitutes apocalyptic literature, this definition has become the standard from which scholars deviate. Scholars have identified a group of revelatory texts, biblical and extra-biblical, that are made up of the characteristics referenced in the SBL study group's definition: first person narrative accounts of visions that use highly symbolic language, have angelic guides, reveal heaven or salvation, and are marked by dualism. John Collins suggests that the three main characteristics of apocalyptic texts are a narrative framework, mediated revelation, and eschatological content.[8]

Many texts share these features, and they come from varying time periods and cultures. Scholars recognize different categories of texts within this newly discovered genre: OT canonical

---

[7] Adela Yarbro Collins, "Introduction: Early Christian Apocalypticism," *Semeia* 36 (1986): 7.

[8] John Collins, *Daniel with an Introduction to Apocalyptic Literature* (Eerdmans, 1984), 4.

apocalypses, OT apocryphal apocalypses, the NT Apocalypse, and Jewish-Christian apocryphal apocalypses.[9] Richard Taylor clarifies how these texts help us: "Non-biblical apocalyptic writings have much in common with their biblical counterparts in terms of interests, concerns, style, themes, and purpose."[10] The search for literary continuity in apocalyptic texts has borne fruit.

Drawing on these studies scholars have slightly nuanced the original SBL study group's definition. For example, Peter Gentry identifies six features of apocalyptic literature: narrative framework, worldview with a schematization of history, revelation given by a heavenly messenger, perspective with a God's-eye view of history, use of colorful metaphors and symbols, and the presentation of future hope in the midst of present trouble.[11] When comparing these variations in defining apocalyptic we see that the main genre features of apocalyptic have been almost universally accepted.

Given these shared literary characteristics, we may propose a scale of apocalyptic literature. The more apocalyptic features a text contains, the more apocalyptic the text is.[12] The need for a scale of apocalyptic explains why there is so much disagreement on what exactly constitutes the genre itself, and why there is no consensus on precisely which biblical texts are apocalyptic.[13] Many prophetic

---

9 John Peter Lange, *The Revelation St. John*, trans. Philip Schaff (Scribner & Sons, 1874), 8.

10 Taylor, *Interpreting Apocalyptic Literature*, 27. Kenton Sparks has identified Mesopotamian, Egyptian, Persian, and Greek apocalyptic works that have patterns similar to potentially apocalyptic OT works: Kenton Sparks, *Ancient Texts for the Study of the Hebrew Bible* (Baker Academic, 2005), 240–251. Some of these are proto-apocalyptic in that they only display a few of features that will characterize later apocalyptic texts. Craig Evans catalogued non-canonical works that predate the NT book of Revelation and are important for interpreting Revelation: Craig Evans, *Ancient Texts for New Testament Studies* (Baker Academic, 2005), 29–34. These include primarily Jewish apocalypses: 1 Enoch, part of the Sybaline Oracles, the Treatise of Shem, the Apocryphon of Ezekiel, the Apocalypse of Zephaniah, and 4 Ezra.

11 Peter Gentry, *How to Read and Understand the Biblical Prophets* (Crossway, 2017), 99.

12 Cf. Taylor, *Interpreting Apocalyptic Literature*, 28. This is also helpful in delineating proto-apocalyptic literature from literature that is highly apocalyptic.

13 D. Brent Sandy suggests 28 features of apocalyptic literature. The seven literary features listed below are the most common, and therefore demand

passages reveal the transcendent reality of salvation, but they do not show enough of the features listed above to warrant being officially labeled apocalyptic. In this work we will focus on preaching biblical passages that are highly apocalyptic, meaning that they share at least four genre markers from the SBL definition. When we look for biblical passages that have these features, we find the following highly apocalyptic passages: Isaiah 6:1–13; Ezekiel 1:1–3:15; 8:1–11:24; 37:1–14; 40:1–48:35; Daniel 7:1–12:13; Zechariah 1:7–6:15; Revelation 1:9–22:20.[14]

The existence of so many texts that share common features warrants the conclusion that apocalyptic literature is a sub-genre of prophetic literature found in both the OT and NT. Not all prophecy is apocalyptic, but all apocalyptic works can be classified as prophecy. The apocalyptic texts in the OT and NT all occur as part of a greater prophetic work. In some cases, like Revelation, the apocalyptic parts of the book are dominant. Apocalyptic visions serve to advance the message of the prophetic works in which they occur. Recognizing apocalyptic literature as a subset of prophecy is essential to grasp each text's contribution to the larger prophetic whole.[15]

Literary Features of Apocalyptic Literature

Equipped with a better understanding of what constitutes apocalyptic literature, we may now identify seven literary features of apocalyptic that guide us in interpreting apocalyptic passages and crafting sermons on them:

1. *Apocalyptic is narrative*—Apocalyptic texts contain a vision report in a first-person narrative. In the vision a prophet or

---

the most attention. D. Brent Sandy, *Plowshares and Pruning Hooks* (InterVarsity, 2002), 109.

14 The genre of Revelation is debated because it shares epistolary features as well as apocalyptic. The letters to the seven churches occur within the greater framework of the apocalyptic vision, which was circulated as an epistle.

15 Andreas J. Kostenberger and Richard D. Patterson, *Invitation to Biblical Interpretation* (Kregel, 2011), 518; D. Brent Sandy, *Plowshares and Pruning Hooks* (InterVarsity, 2002), 107.

apostle is taken on a visionary journey and tells the story of that journey.
2. *Apocalyptic narrative is marked by specific characterization*—The revelation is given to a prophet and explained by an "other-worldly being" (usually an angel, but sometimes God himself).
3. *Apocalyptic texts use aural features to emphasize the message*—These texts were read aloud, and therefore often use literary devices that target the ears of the hearer.
4. *Apocalyptic makes use of signs/symbols*—These visions make use of signs, symbols, figurative characters, and numbers. Some of these may be intentionally bizarre and shocking to the reader for rhetorical effect (think political cartoons).
5. *Apocalyptic contains the revelation of heavenly realities*—Apocalyptic reveals the transcendent reality of the ultimate salvation of God's people and the reality of heaven in a vision. Often this will include a clear delineation of good and evil, and a focus on the victory of God and his people. These visions allow the recipients to reinterpret their difficult circumstances in light of God's ultimate plan and in turn calls them to specific changes in belief/behavior. Apocalyptic literature is meant to be devotional, not merely entertaining.
6. *Apocalyptic serves the greater literary context*—These visions are a subset of prophetic works and must be interpreted and applied in light of their literary context. Additionally, they occur in the literary context of the canon of Scripture and should be preached in light of their contribution to the whole.
7. *Apocalyptic aims for specific rhetorical effects*—The six literary features listed above serve a greater rhetorical purpose. In sermon preparation we must identify the rhetorical purposes of apocalyptic and account for them in our sermons.

The Game Plan

Preparing a sermon on biblical apocalyptic literature requires preparation. The literary characteristics of apocalyptic are built-in guides: they help the preacher discern the main point of these visions. Thus, each chapter in this work is divided into two sections: interpretive insights and homiletic strategies.

In the first part of each chapter, we will identify interpretive insights on one of the seven literary features of apocalyptic—aids to catching the vision. Rather than a full-scale discussion of hermeneutics, these insights briefly highlight important or controversial aspects of interpreting apocalyptic texts.

Then, in the second part of each chapter, we will consider homiletic strategies for casting the vision—crafting sermons in light of the interpretive insights of the given literary feature. In this sense we are following the lead of Fred Craddock who encourages preachers to stay close to the genre of the text: "If the minister wants the sermon to do what the text does, then he or she will want to hold on to the form, since form captures and conveys function, not only during the interpretation of the text but during the designing of the sermon as well."[16]

Before getting into the details, it is important to lay down some homiletical framework. When it comes to specific sermon preparation strategies the approach of this study is based on recognizing the distinction between the exegetical main idea of a preaching portion and a homiletical main idea. The exegetical main idea is a direct result of textual analysis, and ideally would accurately represent the content and purpose of the text. The homiletical main idea is a refinement of the exegetical idea for communication to the congregation or audience in light of the message of the canon. The homiletical main idea should lean towards relevant application of the text to the contemporary audience. In the homiletical main idea, the preacher packages the message of the text with a specific preaching venue in mind.[17]

To prepare to cast the vision we will survey seven literary features of apocalyptic. In Chapters One and Two we will identify the narrative structure of apocalyptic visions that will enable

---

16 Fred B. Craddock, *Preaching* (Abingdon, 1985), 123.

17 For a basic introduction to this concept see Chapter 4 in Haddon R. Robinson, *Biblical Preaching,* 1st ed. (Baker, 1996), 77–106. For a refinement of Robinson's process considering genre awareness see Randal Pelton, *Preaching with Accuracy* (Kregel, 2014). We will discuss considering the homiletical message of apocalyptic in light of the canon of Scripture in Chapter 6.

you to stay on track in crafting a sermon on apocalyptic. Chapter One considers apocalyptic visions as a special kind of narrative: a first-person vision report. Chapter Two looks at the characters who participate in these visions with a focus on the heavenly mediators and the prophetic journeyman.

One often overlooked aspect of communication in apocalyptic visions is the aural effect, which we will listen for in Chapter Three. When preaching apocalyptic, often the hardest parts are the signs, symbols, and numbers. Chapter Four deals with these unusual components in apocalyptic visions by following guides who have helped clarify how to interpret and apply them. These tend to be the most exegetically controversial features of apocalyptic literature. Even so, we will see that the way differing theological systems interpret some of these features may not result in dramatic homiletic differences.

Chapter Five examines the worldview component in apocalyptic visions. These remarkable visions are designed to change us; they transform our interpretation of the world. Apocalyptic brings the good versus evil battle into the forefront. In this chapter we also look at the revolutionary purpose of apocalyptic visions—how each vision is designed to help its readers reinterpret their circumstances.

The final two chapters expand our focus by looking at contextual considerations and the rhetorical effects of apocalyptic. As we prepare sermons on apocalyptic, we need to keep one eye on the overall literary context. Chapter Six examines the placement of apocalyptic visions in the context of the canonical form of the book in which they occur and within the canon of Scripture. Finally, Chapter Seven aims to keep the effects of apocalyptic in view by examining the rhetorical purpose of apocalyptic. Here we underline the importance of asking the "So what?" question in sermon preparation on apocalyptic texts.

My hope is that this work will help catch and cast the vision in preaching on biblical apocalyptic literature. Our goal is to preach well by allowing the unique shape of apocalyptic visions to guide the shape of our sermons.

For Further Study

Arthurs, Jeffrey. *Preaching with Variety.* Kregel Academic, 2007.
Gentry, Peter. *How to Read and Understand the Biblical Prophets.* Crossway, 2017.
Pate, C. Marvin. *Interpreting Revelation and Other Apocalyptic Literature.* Kregel, 2016.
Rogers, Cornish R., and Joseph R. Jeter, Jr. *Preaching through the Apocalypse: Sermons from Revelation.* Chalice, 1992.
Taylor, Richard. *Interpreting Apocalyptic Literature.* Kregel, 2016.

Talk about It

If you've preached on biblical apocalyptic texts before, what was your experience like? What did you find to be the most difficult part of preparing sermons on biblical apocalyptic? Why do you think many preachers hesitate to preach on these texts?

Dig Deeper

While apocalyptic literature is unique, it is by no means beyond our comprehension. This genre is scary to many, but with a little effort and exposure you can gain confidence in both interpreting and preaching these important passages. Consider taking the first steps by reading the works cited above by Richard Taylor and Marvin Pate on interpreting apocalyptic.

Practice

Take notes on a sermon on an apocalyptic vision. Try an internet search of some of your favorite preachers or review sermons in *Preaching through the Apocalypse* cited above. What are ways the preacher's sermon was influenced by the shape of the text? What did you notice that was particularly effective or helpful? Start thinking about how you will approach preaching biblical apocalyptic literature.

1

Apocalyptic as Narrative: Every Vision is a Story

> *All sorrows can be borne if you put them in a story or tell a story about them.*[1]
> Isak Dinesen

At its core, apocalyptic literature is story. Above all their other literary features, these texts contain the first-person narrative account of a vision, where the vision recipient is taken on a visionary journey. Apocalyptic is not merely the utterance of a divine message; apocalyptic visions are events. The prophet sees, hears, and even interacts with the vision. The prophet is then expected to report that vision to his community, usually both verbally and in writing. These visions are narratives, and as such they have a specific discourse structure; apocalyptic literature is a distinct kind of narrative.

Preachers must "attach themselves" to the texts of Scripture we are preaching. This means staying close to the structure of the text in sermon preparation. In preaching apocalyptic it means sticking to the story of the vision. Given that apocalyptic visions are a special expression of narrative, our first strategies for preaching these texts involve staying anchored to the text by discerning and appreciating the narrative structure. The main idea of a sermon on an apocalyptic text should be strongly linked to the main idea of the narrated vision.

---

1 Quoted in Hannah Arendt, *The Human Condition*, 2nd ed. (University of Chicago Press, 1958), 175.

Interpretive Insights

The narrative component of apocalyptic literature is often missed in the homiletic process. To get to know apocalyptic literature as a genre we need to understand it as a special kind of narrative. On one hand, the preacher has a massive amount of resources to help interpret narrative literature in the Bible.[2] On the other hand, virtually none of those resources treat apocalyptic visions as a kind of narrative. The story framework is easy to lose sight of as preachers focus on interpreting elements of the vision, correlating those elements within an eschatological grid, and finding appropriate application for the audience. In order to allow the genre to guide us in sermon preparation, we need to keep the narrative backbone of these texts in view; we need to find the story.

Find the Story: Identifying Flat Narrative Plots

As Leland Ryken observed, narratives "are always built out of three basic ingredients: setting, character, and plot (action). Reading a story involves paying attention to the interaction of these three elements."[3] Apocalyptic visions are first person narratives often with long chunks of description between narrative events.

In apocalyptic visions we find two different kinds of narrative: flat and climactic. A flat narrative has no recorded problem, and therefore has characters who are not involved in any meaningful action; they are simply observers. In these visions the problem must be deduced by the vision or inferred from the explanation of the vision's meaning. The action of the narrative is the prophet witnessing the sign or figures in the vision and the mediator's explanation of what it means. The main exegetical idea of a flat narrative will be either found in the vision mediator's explanation of the vision (when present), or simply in consideration of the vision as a whole.

---

[2] Leland Ryken, *How to Read the Bible as Literature* (Zondervan, 1984); Simon Bar-Efrat, *Narrative Art in the Bible* (T&T Clark, 2004); and Robert Alter, *The Art of Biblical Narrative,* rev. and updated ed. (Basic Books, 2011).

[3] Ryken, *How to Read*, 35.

Zechariah 5:1–4 is a prime example of a flat apocalyptic narrative. After a brief introduction (5:1a), Zechariah sees a flying scroll (5:1b–2). Then the angelic vision guide explains that the scroll represents a curse going out to judge all those who have broken the law. He explains that the scroll will enter the house of hypocrites and destroy (5:3–4). In this case, the main exegetical idea is something like: "God will judge the hidden sin of Israel." The narrative events are limited to Zechariah seeing the scroll, and the brief conversation between him and the angel. There is no real climax. Instead, the meaning of the vision is found in the explanation of the sign.

Equipped with an exegetical idea informed by the narrative structure, the preacher can now craft a homiletical main idea. Move from the exegetical to homiletical main idea here by asking: "How does this passage affect contemporary hearers?"[4] In this example a homiletical main idea could be "God will judge hidden sin."

Find the Story: Identifying Climactic Narrative Plots

The second kind of apocalyptic narrative is climactic. Climactic narratives follow the standard narrative plot arch and have some kind of climax, though the contents of the narrative are primarily visionary rather than literal happenings. The narrative will have an introduction/setting, plot advancement or inciting incident(s), climax, and denouement/resolution. Where do we find the main exegetical idea in a climactic narrative?

In apocalyptic climactic narratives the main idea of the vision will be related to the climax of the narrative. Randy Pelton has provided a helpful method for allowing genre to determine the primary message of a sermon. Regarding narratives he suggests identifying the main idea using the narrative arch: "the background and rising action will yield the subject; climax and conclusion yield the complement to that subject...."[5] When we identify the narrative

---

4 In Chapter 7 we will consider the application of the rhetorical purposes of apocalyptic to contemporary audiences.

5 Randal Pelton, *Preaching with Accuracy* (Kregel, 2014), 62. Pelton

structure, we can home in on the narrative's main idea in the plot by identifying the climax.

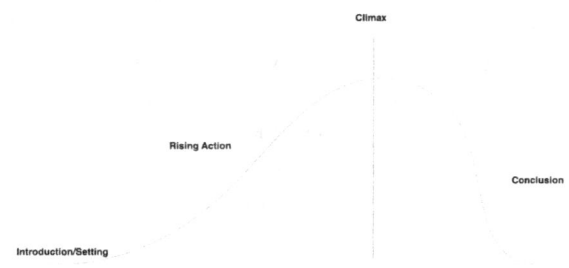

Climactic Narrative Plot Graph

We find additional help identifying the exegetical main idea in apocalyptic narratives where an angelic mediator offers an interpretation of the revelation. In these visions the main idea will be clarified in the interpretation given. In apocalyptic visions Pelton suggests taking the subject and complement of the main idea from the interpretation of the mediator.[6] Naturally it is the actual meaning of the elements in the vision that make up the primary focus, rather than the vision itself. One homiletic misstep in preaching apocalyptic is identifying the exegetical idea without reference to the vision-mediator's interpretation. For example, Taylor's analysis of the main exegetical idea of the vision of Daniel 8 misses the mark: "An angel explains to Daniel the significance of a vision in which Daniel sees a powerful goat overpowering a two-horned ram and a little horn causing even greater destruction,"[7] but what does the angel say it means?

Taking into account the angelic interpretation in Daniel 8:17–26, the exegetical main idea would be: "An angel explains to Daniel that the vision of a goat overpowering a two-horned ram and a little horn causing even greater destruction refers to the Medo-Persian

---

distinguishes between the textual big idea and homiletic big idea. My key takeaway from Pelton here is that we cannot craft a homiletic main idea without discerning the textual big idea in light of the narrative structure.

6 Ibid., 77–78.

7 Richard A. Taylor, *Interpreting Apocalyptic Literature* (Kregel, 2016), 164.

and Greek empires, along with the remnants of the Greek empire, causing persecution of Israel."

Take Ezekiel's second vision as an example of an apocalyptic vision with a climactic narrative (Ezek 8:1–11:25). In the introduction, Ezekiel travels in a vision to the temple in Jerusalem (8:1–4). The progress of the plot line clarifies the topic of the narrative: he witnesses Israel's leaders worshipping false gods at the temple of the Lord (8:5–18). The climax of the vision occurs as God judges Jerusalem and the glory of the Lord departs from the temple (9:1–11:23). God commands Ezekiel to prophesy (in the vision!) against the idolatrous elders of Israel while giving a message of hope to those already in exile. In the conclusion he returns to the exiles (11:24–25).

The narrative discourse structure yields the following exegetical outline:

I. Introduction: Ezekiel 8:1–4
II. Plot/Conflict: Ezekiel 8:5–18 (main topic subject)
III. Climax: Ezekiel 9:1–11:23 (main topic predicate)
IV. Conclusion: Ezekiel 11:24–25

So, the main exegetical idea of the vision would be something like: "Israel's idolatry caused the Lord to leave the temple and judge his people, but not without the hope of restoration." Moving from exegetical to homiletical main idea, we might choose something like: "Every idol is incompatible with the presence of God, but we find hope in God's redeeming promises." The specific wording is not as important as the link between the primary message of the sermon and the primary message of these unique narratives.

Commissioning visions are a special subset of climactic apocalyptic narratives. These narratives follow the normal plot pattern, and they share a common inciting conflict: the sinfulness or unworthiness of the vision recipient and his people. This problem is resolved by direct intervention or assurance from God or an angel, and the result is God commissioning the prophet to deliver his message to the people. Isaiah 6:1–14, Ezekiel 1:1–3:14, and Revelation 1:9–20 are all climactic commissioning narratives.

A possible exegetical main idea for Isaiah's commissioning narrative is: "Isaiah's seeing the Lord enthroned in his heavenly temple is followed by the Lord providing atonement for Isaiah's sin and sending him as a prophet to Israel." Note that this exegetical main idea follows the flow of the commissioning narrative: the problem is Isaiah's (and his people's) sin, and the climax is found in provision of atonement from the coal from the altar. One way to express a homiletical main idea from this text is: "God's purifying grace is our only hope for restoration."

In Revelation 1:9–20 the apostle John is commissioned to deliver Jesus's words to the seven churches of Asia Minor. Revelation 1:9–11 is the introduction as John explains the start of the vision. In 1:12–17a the plot progresses as he sees a revelation of Jesus and falls on his face as a dead man. In the climax (1:17b–20) Jesus comforts him and explains what the golden lamp-stand and stars represent. The main focus of the text is in the explanation, that Jesus died and rose from the dead and is the central focus of the seven churches. One option for a homiletic main idea is: "The risen Savior reigns over the risen church."

Enjoy the View: Exposition Embedded in Vision Reports

Another unique element of apocalyptic first-person narratives is the presence of long explanatory sections. Chunks of descriptive exposition can make the narrative component of each vision easy to miss. These sections are lengthy descriptions of what the prophet is seeing, or lengthy explanations by the vision mediator. Far from being irrelevant, these descriptions help to clarify the main topic of the vision and points of emphasis.[8] The language in these descriptive passages is vivid, allowing the reader to envision what the prophet is seeing and hearing.

Ezekiel's first vision is a commissioning narrative complete with a long explanatory section where he describes his vision of

---

[8] Grammatically these chunks of exposition are normally different from the narrative backbone of the apocalyptic text. E.g., in Hebrew apocalyptic texts the primary narrative verb form will be a *wayyiqtol* while in exposition it will be a *yiqtol* or *weqatal*.

the throne room of God (Ezek 1:1–3:14). After the introduction in 1:1–3, Ezekiel sees the throne room of God revealed in a storm. The key plot problem here is Israel's sin, which is introduced after the throne room description (1:4–2:5). God then calls Ezekiel to proclaim his word to Israel, with the caveat that they will not respond well. As a symbol of his role, Ezekiel is told to eat a scroll, and the message is repeated (2:6–3:13). The vision concludes with Ezekiel returning to where he started and then spending a week in stunned reflection on the vision (3:14–15).

The description of the throne of God is significant in this commissioning narrative as it takes up one third of the entire vision. Such textual real estate is an indication of importance. At the time the vision was given to Ezekiel, Israel was in exile in Babylon. Israel in exile was a spiritually disenfranchised people, and the question of God's sovereignty loomed large, especially in the early days of exile. Was God sovereign? The beginning of Ezekiel's vision settles that question right away. Ezekiel 1:4–2:5 is so prominent, in fact, it may warrant a sermon in and of itself. The exegetical main idea here might be something like: "God's sovereign reign is still in force even while Israel is in exile." From there a homiletic big idea might be something like: "God is always on his throne even when it doesn't seem like it."

Often the description or explanation of the angelic vision mediator is key to understanding the main focus of the vision. These interpretations are a gift to the preacher, as they remove any doubt as to what important signs mean in the vision and what is key for the prophet to understand. In sermons on these visions the main idea should be framed in light of the authorized interpretation. Taylor helpfully warns against over-interpretation of apocalyptic visions, highlighting the need to focus on the interpretation given rather than supply missing information: "In apocalyptic literature the level of detail provided in figurative analogies is usually greater than the level of detail provided in their interpretation. Not every feature in an illustration necessarily has a corresponding feature in the interpretation."[9]

Daniel's vision in Daniel 9:20–27 is an example of a vision

---

9 Taylor, *Interpreting Apocalyptic Literature*, 124.

made up entirely of an angelic explanation. Daniel 9:20–21 is the introduction where Daniel explains how the angel Gabriel came to him while he was praying. Daniel 9:22–23 contains the angel Gabriel's explanation that what he is about to reveal is an answer to Daniel's prayer. Daniel 9:24–27 contain the revelation about the 70 weeks of years, focusing on the goal of removing Israel's sin and bringing about prosperity. The exegetical main idea here might be: "Gabriel reveals the coming 70 'sevens' to Daniel, during which sin will be removed by atonement and the temple will be established in contrast to the state of Jerusalem and the temple during Daniel's lifetime." A possible homiletical big idea for this vision is: "God provides the lasting solution to the problem of sin."

Homiletical Strategy 1: Tell the Story

If a sermon on a biblical apocalyptic text reflects the shape of that text, the sermon must tell the story. We need not reinvent the wheel here. Allow the natural flow of the narrative arc of the vision to guide the form of the sermon. One way to do this is to use the four stages of a narrative as a skeleton for the sermon structure: background, conflict/plot, climax, and conclusion. The preacher needs to communicate the circumstances of the original audience (background), summarize the vision narrative in some fashion and articulate why the vision was relevant to them and how it is relevant today (rising action), focus on how the conflict is resolved (climax), and provide some concrete takeaways for the real world (conclusion). One advantage to using the narrative arc as the form for the sermon is it naturally follows the text of the vision.

Set the Stage

First, introduce the background. If setting is the starting point for any story, then a sermon on an apocalyptic text needs to establish the setting of the prophet and original audience. Think of this as the opening of a movie where a few short sentences or brief montage catch the viewer up to speed so that they can make sense of the story. What were the circumstances of the original readers?

Setting the stage by summarizing the suffering of the original audience helps the modern audience start to make sense of why such fantastic visions were helpful and even necessary.

Setting the scene can be done creatively, using this time as a chance to capture the audience's attention. It can also be done with efficient brevity. Consider offering a few helpful nuggets of historical background. In many cases the situation of the first readers is beyond dispute (Ezekiel, Zechariah, Revelation), and therefore the preacher can quickly bring the audience up to speed. Even in texts where scholars disagree about the date of origin, as in Daniel, the original audience was still experiencing a crisis of faith—either in exile or under the persecution of Antiochus IV. Without going into scholarly detail, the preacher can establish that the original recipients were in a crisis of faith and/or experiencing persecution.

This necessary background/setting portion of a sermon should never evolve into a history lecture. By using one of several homiletic techniques a preacher can effectively communicate essential information without putting people to sleep. For example, consider using an effective visual aid that summarizes the setting. Key dates on a timeline or pictorial representations of events can be helpful ways to keep people engaged. Or try using a creative narrative re-telling of the original readers' circumstances as a way to build interest. For example, in preaching Ezekiel 1:1–3:15 you could say:

> Ezekiel's generation was forced to march away from a nation already in spiritual crisis. A few years after arriving in Babylon they would hear of the destruction of Jerusalem and the burning of the temple of the Lord. This would have left a 9/11 kind of emotional scar on each exile. They would have been wondering, where is God in all this? Has he abandoned us? Maybe the gods of Babylon are stronger than the Lord.

Rising Action

Second, highlight the conflict. Communicating the background paves the way for identifying the main problem in the plot. Setting the scene sets up the preacher to address the crucial question of why this vision for these people. Why is it tethered to their specific experiences? Daniel's vision of the 70 weeks of years in chapter 9 is occasioned by his prayer in light of the fact that Israel had been in exile in Babylon for about 70 years. He prayed for God's mercy in light of the time of exile drawing to an end. But was the problem that caused the exile in the first place really resolved? The vision of the 70 weeks answers no, but it will be.

In telling the story let the stages of advancement of the plot influence the progress of the sermon. The building of tension in the vision narrative is a natural way to increase interest in the audience. While their circumstances are not the same as the original audience, they will still share similar feelings. As David Jacobsen said: "Apocalyptic texts come to us not because we are their first addressees (we're not), but because apocalyptic texts do something with the way we view the world."[10] Pate refers to this process as identifying the shared need. He suggests two steps to connect ancient circumstances to modern needs: "isolate the need(s) addressed in the historical and literary context of the passage; determine the need(s) contemporary listeners share with the original audience."[11] After explaining the problem for the original audience, explain how that is relevant to the congregation.

Eugene Lowry's focus on induction in *The Homiletical Plot* is helpful here. He writes: "The homiletical plot must catch people in the depths of the awful discrepancies on their world—social and personal."[12] Telling the story of apocalyptic visions is a counter-intuitive way to help modern hearers consider the challenges and crises that they are facing. Think of this as history telling with a specific purpose. Continuing our example from Ezekiel 1–3 above, we might add:

> Have you ever been there? To that place where you wonder if

---

10 David Schnasa Jacobsen, *Preaching in the New Creation, the Promise of New Testament Apocalyptic Texts* (Westminster John Knox, 1999), 16. We will consider the reality of two contexts in application in Chapter 7.

11 C. Marvin Pate, *Interpreting Revelation and Other Apocalyptic Literature* (Kregel, 2016), 174. We will return to the topic of making appropriate application in Chapter 7.

12 Eugene L. Lowry, *The Homiletical Plot* (Westminster John Knox, 2001).

God is really on his throne? Maybe it was in a doctor's office when you got that diagnosis, or at home when you opened that unexpected bill, or at school when your closest friend betrayed you. Perhaps as a church we look at developments in our culture and ask that very question. We all face those moments of spiritual crisis, but what Israel needed, and what we need, is to know God as he is.

Climax and Solution

Third, focus on the climax and resolution of the problem (and the explanation of the vision by the angelic guide, if present). In the example of Isaiah's commissioning narrative vision, the climax of the vision is the provision of purification for Isaiah by the burning coal from the altar touching his lips. It is only God's provision of atonement that enables a sinful man/people to remain in his presence. A sermon on this vision should focus on that climactic moment. We will consider the question of how to address the canonical relevance in Chapter Six, but at this point note that the sermon should give weight to the main focus of the vision. In this specific example the holiness of God is an important part of the vision, but not the main focus. A sermon on Isaiah 6:1–14 should reflect the vision's emphasis on atonement and explain how that relates to the contemporary hearer. You might say:

> We may not be called to be an OT prophet, but we are from a people of unclean lips in need of purification by an atoning sacrifice. In light of the holiness of our majestic God we see our sinfulness with clarity. Woe am I! Woe are we! Yet we need not wallow in despair. God has provided grace for us through sacrifice. What Israel needed—what we need—is not greater will power to do better. They needed forgiveness. We need forgiveness. The burning coal from the altar here anticipates a greater sacrifice: the sacrifice of Jesus, the Messiah. His death and resurrection are the only way anyone can be welcomed into the temple of thrice holy God. God's purifying grace is our only hope for restoration.

Finally, conclude a sermon on apocalyptic by reminding the audience of practical takeaways they will need. Often apocalyptic visions end with the vision recipient returning to the real world with the message. In one sense, the conclusion of the sermon is that moment for the congregation. After embarking on a journey through the vision, they now must re-enter their atmosphere. Help them by highlighting two or three practical ways the text enables them to walk by faith.

Summary of Homiletical Strategy 1

Keeping the narrative main idea is key in crafting a sermon on an apocalyptic text. Careful study of the narrative structure and awareness of unique features like long explanatory sections helps the preacher focus on the primary emphasis of the vision. One major pitfall in preaching biblical apocalyptic literature is allowing the main idea of a sermon to stray too far from the main idea of the vision itself. The preacher needs the homiletic discipline to ask: "Does this sermon emphasize what the vision emphasizes?" Telling the story also requires us to bring the audience up to speed regarding the setting of the vision in question, helping them to grasp why the vision was helpful then, and how it might be helpful to them now. Use the natural narrative arc of the vision to structure a sermon that flows with the text.

Homiletical Strategy 2: Divide the Text Appropriately

A second homiletic strategy informed by reading apocalyptic as narrative is dividing the text appropriately. Breaking up apocalyptic texts for preaching falls into two broad categories: dividing a text into chunks for one particular sermon or dividing a vision or a series of visions into sections for a preaching series. In both tasks, identifying the narrative structure of apocalyptic texts allows the preacher to divide the text into sections that are appropriate for the ministry context of the sermon.

While a few apocalyptic visions are very short (e.g., Zechariah 5:1–4), some are long. Ezekiel's fourth vision encompasses nine chapters in Ezekiel 40:1–48:35. The variety in the size of apocalyptic texts means we must give careful attention to dividing the text appropriately. To do this we must ask a few key questions. How long will the sermon or series be? How much text will I plan to read in a given sermon? How familiar will my audience be with the text? Like carving a road through a mountain pass, we need to follow the natural contours in apocalyptic visions as we parcel out the text and budget sermon time.

Getting Used to Apocalyptic Vision Narratives

When we take time getting comfortable with biblical apocalyptic literature, the usual components become clear: a vision recipient receives a vision, is taken somewhere, an angelic guide or mediator helps them understand the key points of the vision, and they return to their point of origin. Other frequent elements include longer sections of description or explanation, and the prophet's response to the vision. The specific components of a vision are the starting point for dividing up the text into manageable chunks for a sermon. As Randy Pelton writes: "Most of the time the beginning and ending of a particular vision identify a valid preaching portion (cf. Revelation 4:1–11)."[13]

The most natural way to divide up an apocalyptic text is to follow the narrative plot development. As we saw in strategy one, the setting of the vision may provide a seamless way to introduce tension and highlight needs in the audience that the vision will address. Moving on from the introduction, track the plot progression and deal with the particular problems that advance the vision. These problems will lead to a focus in the sermon on the climax or vision explanation.

For example, in Ezekiel's second vision the main problem is the idolatry of Israelites in Jerusalem. The introduction/setting to the vision is 8:1–4. As we have already seen, the plot progresses with the revelation of idolatry in 8:5–18. This section includes four different examples of Israel's idolatry. In 9:1–11 the Lord responds to

---

13 Pelton, *Preaching with Accuracy,* 55. He goes on to note the importance of including the interpretation with the vision.

Israel's idolatry by sending an angel to judge Jerusalem. The climax of the vision occurs in 10:1–11:23 as Ezekiel witnesses the glory of the Lord departing from the temple. The vision concludes in 11:24–25 as Ezekiel is returned to the exiles. The chunks of text in the plot progression and climax are long enough to be independent sermons, or they could be summarized as parts of one sermon.

If you decide on a preaching portion that does not include the climax of the vision narrative or the mediator's explanation of the vision, be sure to be aware of the overall main exegetical idea from those sections. Ezekiel 8 lends itself well to a consideration of different kinds of idolatry, but the key idea in the vision narrative is the resulting departure of God's glory from Israel and his judgment. One pitfall in preaching apocalyptic visions is neglecting the exegetical main idea. Difficult though it may be, we are better served to approach these passages with discipline and limit our proclamation to what God has said in the text. Richard Taylor makes this point well, offering this caution on going too far with apocalyptic visions: "Faithful interpretation means that we respect the silence of the biblical text and refuse to go beyond what the text itself affirms. Where the text is silent, we must learn to live with that silence."[14]

The temptation to over-interpret details of apocalyptic visions is not limited to one eschatological viewpoint. Luther had no doubt that the Antichrist was the pope:

> This matter shows irrefutably that he is the true end-times Antichrist, who has raised himself over and set himself against Christ, because the pope does not allow Christians to be saved without his authority, which, nevertheless, amounts to nothing and is not ordered or commanded by God.[15]

Even the eminent theologian Jonathan Edwards identified the false prophet of Revelation 16:14 as possibly the pope, but more likely Mohammed, the founder of Islam:

---

14 Taylor, *Interpreting Apocalyptic Literature*, 127.
15 Martin Luther, "The Smalcald Articles," in *The Annotated Luther*, ed. Kirsi I. Stjerna, (Fortress, 2015), 2:440.

...by the false prophet, is sometimes meant the pope and his clergy; but here an eye seems to be had to Mahomet, whom his followers call the great prophet of God.[16]

In the 1930s many premillennial interpreters speculated on how nations in current events mapped onto prophesies, including apocalyptic visions. Alva McClain identified the "king of the south" in Daniel 11:40 as the king of England.[17] Each of these dubious identifications has proven inaccurate, and collectively they serve as a warning against overzealous identification of signs and symbols in apocalyptic.

If you are planning to read the entire text of one vision throughout a sermon, be mindful that the main idea and focus will likely be in the angelic explanation of the vision or the climax of the vision narrative. Both of these will occur in the latter portion of the text, and therefore you will need to allow sufficient time to focus on them. Watch out for spending too much time on the vision and not leaving enough for the interpretation by the angelic guide. Consider revealing key parts of the vision at the beginning of a sermon, like this example in the case of Revelation 1:9–20:

> As we look at this vision you need to keep in mind that the golden lampstands represent the seven churches that were John's first audience. Watch for where Jesus is standing in relation to the lampstands.

If you do not plan to read the entire text, you may still want to structure the sermon in light of the narrative progression. Allow the circumstances of the original recipients to influence which problems in the modern audience you address. Identify key verses in each section, perhaps giving time to each one as you progress. Be sure to explain any central visionary elements, and to clarify any translation confusion.

---

16 Jonathan Edwards, "A History of the Work of Redemption," in *Works of Jonathan Edwards: Volume One* (The Banner of Truth Trust, 1995), 606, electronic ed.

17 Alva J. McClain, "The Four Great Powers of the End-Time," *The King's Business* 29 (Feb 1938): 100.

It may be helpful to let the audience know that while we may not know all the details about the visionary elements in the passage, we do know what the Lord has provided through the mediating angels. When present, these angelic explanations function as a Spirit-inspired vision interpretation aide. They also help the preacher not get too distracted in dealing with matters of eschatological speculation.[18]

Induction vs. Deduction

An important consideration when dividing apocalyptic texts for preaching is determining whether the sermon will be inductive or deductive. A deductive sermon states the main point or idea at the beginning, and then demonstrates that point from the biblical passages.[19] An inductive sermon in one in which the key question or need is introduced early in the sermon and the main point is reserved until later.[20] Donald Sunukjian suggests that most biblical texts lend themselves well to an inductive sermon: "Since most biblical passages are themselves inductive, with the author reasoning toward a conclusion or unfolding a story to a climax, we might approach each sermon with a slight bent toward inductive...."[21]

As we have seen, the main idea in apocalyptic visions is situated later in the passage, in the climax or angelic explanation. Therefore, these visions are ideal for the inductive sermon form. If a preacher can introduce the tension or problem and sustain interest throughout the vision itself and explanation, the impact on the hearer can be powerful. When it comes to allowing the shape of the genre to influence the shape of the sermon, the inductive sermon form is ideal.

However, when the subject material of the passages is foreign to modern audiences, a deductive sermon form might be more appropriate to help audiences not lose sight of the main homiletic

---

18 See Chapter 6.
19 Donald R. Sunukjian, *Invitation to Biblical Preaching* (Kregel, 2007), 143.
20 Ibid., 144. He goes on to say: "The complete take-home truth emerges later in the body of the message, whenever the assertion or answer ('what you're saying about it') appears in the biblical flow of thought."
21 Ibid., 160.

idea. Unusual place names, ancient historical settings, and fantastic visionary elements can demand much from sermon listeners. The preacher should consider those who will be in the audience and what sermon form will best serve to communicate to them.

Handling Long Passages

With longer visions, reading the entire passage will not be possible in one sermon. In some cases, the vision may be so significant that it warrants multiple messages. For example, you might do an entire sermon on Ezekiel 1:1–2:5 focusing on the throne room of God, while dealing with the prophetic commissioning of Ezekiel in another sermon on 2:6–3:15. The advantage here is allowing the weightiness of certain aspects of the vision to drive the division of the text for preaching, thus allowing the emphasis in different parts of the vision to be the emphasis of the respective sermons.

In other cases, summarizing the vision will be the only realistic homiletic strategy. Spend time identifying the key passages you want to be sure to read. Also spend time identifying important concepts and repeated themes in the vision. It can be helpful to write out a summary of the parts you will omit, so as to limit rambling or rabbit trails.

If your liturgy or order of service allows, ask someone to read portions of the vision at some point in the service before the sermon. If you are preaching weekly to the same congregation, consider communicating the preaching portions ahead of time and asking people to read it on their own before the sermon. Provide a few application questions to help them prepare for what they will hear in the message.

A Sermon Series on Apocalyptic Literature

If you are brave enough to preach a long series through a prophet like Ezekiel, you will need to be ready to handle the apocalyptic visions among the other prophetic sub-genres. Often preachers tackle Revelation by splitting it into the epistolary and visionary sections, but keep in mind the latter is the bulk of the text. Shorter books like Zechariah lend themselves well to a stand-alone sermon series.

In lieu of an expositional series through a prophet or a series on the visions of a particular prophet, another way to approach preaching apocalyptic visions is to address them thematically. A series based on highlights from Zechariah's visions would be a great way to expose a congregation to the key themes of hope and confidence in God in those visions. An exegetical-topical sermon series on God's sovereignty in Ezekiel's visions would highlight an important theme scattered throughout Ezekiel. The setting right of wrongs and the judgment of the wicked in Revelation is a potential thematic way to approach preaching John's apocalyptic vision.

When it comes to purely thematic or topical sermon series, biblical apocalyptic literature offers many significant contributions. Some important themes in apocalyptic literature are idolatry, God's sovereignty, faithfulness to God in the midst of suffering and persecution, hope in God during trials, God's miraculous work regenerating sinners, the judgment of the wicked and vindication of the righteous, and eternal peace and prosperity for the people of God. In a thematic series, a sermon on an apocalyptic text can add an out of the ordinary and attention-getting alternative to the more familiar genres in the Bible.

Although these visions may offer much to a thematic series, we need to be careful about the difficulty in dropping an audience or congregation into one of these passages cold. Gordon Fee warns about this in preaching from Revelation: "Do not try to preach from the Revelation apart from a series. You simply have to spend too much time explaining things so that a single sermon from the book has any number of pitfalls associated with it."[22] We need to be careful that if we include a one-off sermon on apocalyptic literature, we are well prepared to handle it in a way that helps rather than distracts or confuses the congregation. Preaching Revelation or other apocalyptic literature in a series can be fruitful, but Fee's warning is sound.

---

22 Gordon D. Fee, "Preaching Apocalyptic? You've God to be Kidding!" *CTJ* 41 (2006): 14.

Summary of Homiletical Strategy 2

We should allow the narrative structure of apocalyptic visions to guide the division of apocalyptic texts for sermons and sermon series. Watch for parts of the vision that will require time-consuming explanations and note natural breaks. Be sure to have a firm grasp on the main idea of the vision as revealed in the climax or the heavenly mediator's description. Think creatively about dealing with longer texts, and consider including apocalyptic literature in thematic series. As we faithfully divide the text, we are one step closer to faithfully proclaiming it.

Thus, we begin catching and casting the vision by identifying the narrative backbone of apocalyptic texts. Our two homiletic strategies in light of apocalyptic being a special kind of narrative are to tell the story of the apocalyptic vision, ensuring that we do not obscure the overarching narrative theme, and to divide the text in light of the narrative shape. Sticking close to the text means crafting a sermon informed by the vision's narrative backbone. Once we have identified the narrative arc, the next step is identifying the characters in the story.

For Further Study

Alter, Robert. *The Art of Biblical Narrative*, rev. and updated ed. Basic Books, 2011.
Bar-Efrat, Simon. *Narrative Art in the Bible*. T&T Clark, 2004.
Pelton, Randal. *Preaching with Accuracy*. Kregel, 2014.
Ryken, Leland. *How to Read the Bible as Literature*. Zondervan, 1984.

Talk about It

Read a few apocalyptic visions in Zechariah, Daniel, and Ezekiel to get a sense of the narrative flow. What similarities do you notice? How are these narratives different than a historical narrative?

Dig Deeper

Recognizing the narrative structure of apocalyptic literature is the first step in mastering the genre. Review the basic components of narrative. Perhaps familiarize yourself with Pelton's take on identifying the main exegetical idea in narrative and visionary literature (*Preaching with Accuracy*, 61–68, 77–79).

Practice

Create a narrative outline for Ezekiel 37:1–14. Identify the introduction/setting, the plot progression, and the climax. Focus on the explanation of the symbols in the vision. Using your narrative outline, craft a homiletic outline. Remember that you do not need to recreate the narrative outline exactly, but that it should influence how you think about outlining your sermon.

2

Apocalyptic Characterization: The Cast of Participants in the Vision

> *You can't go far wrong with a story if you simply go through the action as the observant traveling companion of the protagonist in the story.*[1]
> Leland Ryken

IDENTIFYING THE NARRATIVE STRUCTURE of each vision is one key to discerning the design of apocalyptic visions when crafting sermons on them. Another is noting the characterization: clearly identifying the characters in the vision and their contribution to it.

Armed with the knowledge that apocalyptic is a first-person narrative vision report, we need to consider how the prophet and other characters in the vision are presented. Because apocalyptic is a unique kind of narrative, characterization in apocalyptic visions has marked differences from historical narrative. Careful attention to the ways the characters in the vision are presented will equip the preacher to shape the sermon in light of the apocalyptic vision's purpose and presentation.

Like Peter, Susan, Edmund, and Lucy in C.S. Lewis's classic *The Lion, the Witch, and the Wardrobe,* hearers of sermons on apocalyptic texts embark on a journey to a new world. The homiletic strategies that flow out of observing the characterization in apocalyptic visions aim to welcome hearers into the world of the vision. This means the preacher will need to employ the skills of a storyteller and seek to capture the attention and imagination of the congregation.

---

1 Leland Ryken, *How to Read the Bible as Literature* (Zondervan, 1984), 43.

Interpretive Insights

Getting to know the characters in apocalyptic visions (and helping our hearers know them) requires attention to dialogue, action, and physical descriptions in the vision. You will need to introduce people to the heavenly mediator and other characters in the vision, including, sometimes, an antagonist, but the first character to get to know is the prophet, who functions as a special kind of protagonist.

A Special Kind of Protagonist

Each vision recipient is the protagonist of their story, but not a typical protagonist. God sent apocalyptic visions to prophets as representatives of the people. This means the prophet in an apocalyptic vision is a representative protagonist. Jeffrey Arthurs describes how the protagonist is the key figure in a narrative: "The most important person in the story is the protagonist, a term that reminds us that plot and character cannot be separated: 'protagonist' means literally the 'primary struggler.'"[2] But prophets in apocalyptic visions are not traditional protagonists in that they rarely perform the action of the narrative.

If they are not the primary agent in the story, what is their role? The prophet witnesses the vision and participates in it (rather than merely hearing the message from God and delivering it). Michael Fox relates how this participatory element links the prophet to his audience: "By choosing this stance the rhetor steps into the audience, as it were, and aligns himself with them."[3] So Ezekiel not only sees a scroll but eats it. Zechariah sees and has conversations with the various characters in his visions. Daniel fell asleep during one vision and had to be awakened to stand once again. John bowed before an angel, only to be told to get up.

As representative protagonists, these prophets see, hear, and act in the vision for the people. In this regard it is crucial that they also report what happened to them to the people. The vision report

---

[2] Jeffrey Arthurs, *Preaching with Variety* (Kregel Academic, 2007), 72.

[3] F. Michael Fox, "The Rhetoric of Ezekiel's Vision of the Valley of the Bones," *Hebrew Union College Annual* 51 (1980): 9.

must be trustworthy; therefore, the prophet is always a familiar or authorized messenger. The people to whom these visions were given needed hope, and they needed to know that these incredible vision journeys were more than just the figment of someone's imagination.[4] The hopeless or perilous situation of the audiences of these visions meant they needed to see realities going on elsewhere. Thus, the prophet needed to embark on a journey both to different locations on earth (for example, Ezekiel to Jerusalem in Ezekiel 8–11) and/or to the spiritual dimension that they simply could not see. The authorized prophet here offers hope to his audience by relating what happened to him in the vision: what he saw, what he heard, and what he was asked to do. Because a trusted messenger had been taken on this visionary journey, the people could bank on what he had seen.

The Heavenly Mediator

As the authoritative prophet/representative experienced his vision journey, he not only saw the vision, he interacted with the vision guide via dialogue. The prophet as the representative protagonist is the main character in an apocalyptic vision, but every apocalyptic vision also includes the presence of a heavenly mediator. This dialogue often gives key interpretive information or answers questions the prophet may have. The mediator's words will clarify the meaning of symbols that are otherwise unknown to the prophet (or readers).

In some cases, the guide is the Lord himself (for example, Ezekiel 8–11); in others the guide is an angel (this is more common, as in Daniel, Zechariah, and Revelation). Why use a supernatural mediator? John Collins points out that the presence of a heavenly agent alerts the audience to the supernatural forces at work in the world:

> The manner of revelation requires the mediation of an otherworldly being: i.e., it is not given directly to the human

---

[4] Perhaps this is why Daniel's visions are presented after the narrative of his spiritual heroics. He was not a prophet *per se*, and thus his audience needed to know why they could trust him.

recipient and does not fall within the compass of human knowledge. The manner of revelation then already asserts the reality of another world, superior to our own in knowledge, even in the knowledge of human affairs and destiny.[5]

The explanatory speech between the heavenly mediator and the prophet is revelatory. They illuminate a point of view to which the prophet and people do not have access outside of this special revelation. Shimon Bar-Efrat suggests that one purpose of dialogue is to effect change: "Speech directed at someone else is sometimes intended to arouse a certain emotion or attitude in them...."[6] When the heavenly mediator calls the prophet to action or explains the meaning of the vision, he intends to produce a change in attitude and perspective not only for the prophet, but for the people he represents.

For example, in Zechariah's first vision he sees four different colored horses (and presumably riders, cf. Zech 1:7–17). Zechariah asks his guide what they are, and the guide answers, "They are the ones the Lord has sent to patrol the earth" (Zech 1:10). At that point the vision story continues with the report from the riders. The angel then asks how long until the Lord will be merciful to Israel by judging her enemies. He goes on to give Zechariah the main point: he is to tell those who have returned from exile that God will bless Jerusalem and the rebuilding of the temple. In this vision, the narrative is short—Zechariah just sees some horses and riders and hears their report. The guide clarifies the significance of what Zechariah saw and heard. The main exegetical point of the vision would be something like: "God's sovereignty over the nations results in his blessing Israel's resettlement of Jerusalem."

The effect of this dialogue between the prophet and the heavenly mediator is to strengthen the confidence of the audience in the revelation. In these visions the audience is invited to confidently reinterpret their situation on the ground in light of the supernatural truths revealed. If they are suffering, it will not last forever.

---

5 John J. Collins, "Introduction: Towards the Morphology of a Genre," *Semeia* 14 (1979): 10.

6 Shimon Bar-Efrat, *Narrative Art in the Bible* (T&T Clark International, 2004), 70.

If they are persecuted, God will avenge them. If they are going through trials, they have an ultimate purpose.

There Is Only One Hero

While the prophet is the protagonist of apocalyptic visions, he is definitely not the hero. Rather, he is called upon to witness the judgment or salvation of God. There can be no doubt that God is the savior in these visions. Some apocalyptic visions do not picture God acting, but many do. In Daniel 7, the Ancient of Days takes his seat on the throne and judges the kingdoms of the earth (Dan 7:9–10). Also, in Daniel 7 the Son of Man takes his authority over all the kingdoms of the earth (7:13–14). In Zechariah 2:5 the Lord declares that he is the wall of fire protecting Jerusalem. In Revelation 5 and 6 the Lamb takes and opens the scroll of judgement, and in Revelation 19:11–16 Jesus executes judgment riding on a white horse.

This unusual character structure—the prophet as protagonist but God as hero—effectively anchors any hope for believers in God rather than in the prophet or themselves. The message of these visions is not "look to the prophet" or "look within yourselves" but "look to the Lord." God has acted in times past, is active now, and will act in the future. He is the hero, and that is especially relevant when believers seem to be on the losing team.

Supporting Cast

God, the prophetic vision recipient, and the heavenly mediator are not the only characters in these remarkable visions. Leland Ryken notes the unusual nature of the group of characters in apocalyptic visions: "Filling this cosmic stage are actors that do not fit ordinary expectations."[7] In these visions we find fantastic beasts that are mixtures of animals (and even humans), stork-women, demon locusts, various kinds of angels, and a red dragon. Even nature becomes animate as the earth participates in the action in Revelation 12:16.[8]

---

7 Ryken, *How to Read the Bible as Literature*, 168.
8 Ibid., 168.

These other worldly characters contribute to the fantastic imagery of apocalyptic visions. They are crucial props in the attention arresting and shocking nature of the visionary narrative. Every biblical apocalyptic text makes use of stunning characters and shocking images. These images are designed to jar the audience, forcing them to imagine something more than what they are able to see. Ezekiel's vision of God's throne and the valley of the dry bones, Zechariah's woman in a basket and his flying scroll, Daniel's battling animals and descending Son of Man, and John's demon locusts and dragon all easily qualify as shocking images.

The shock factor in the supporting cast helps persuade the audience of their need for a new perspective on their circumstances. Fox says: "Strange, shocking, and bizarre images on the other hand are needed when one seeks to break down old frameworks of perception and to create new ones."[9] Both Ezekiel's and Daniel's visions were given to disenfranchised Israelites in exile. Zechariah's visions were given to Israelites who had returned from exile only to find Jerusalem in shambles. John's visions were given to Christians, who were an often-persecuted minority in Roman Asia Minor in the 1st century AD. In each of these situations, the intended effect of these shocking images is to push the audience to consider the fact that the loss, hopelessness, or trials filling their vision will not have the last word. On the contrary, God is still enthroned and at work in the universe, including their specific situation.

Whether past, present, or future, these shocking images were designed to change the way the audience thinks about a given circumstance by showing them what they could not see. Like a cold bucket of water tossed onto someone peacefully asleep, these shocking characters and images jolt the reader into spiritual alertness. The hearers of these visions quickly realize they do not have all the information. More than that, there is a glorious yet hidden transcendent reality that provides them with hope in the midst of a hopeless circumstance.

The supporting characters represent real entities in the world, and how they act or are acted upon in the vision is instructive for the vision recipients. What they represent is either self-evident or

---

9 Fox, "Rhetoric," 9.

made clear by the heavenly mediator. Those that represent spiritual beings such as angels and demons remind the hearer that at work in the universe are spiritual forces which we do not see. Those that represent nature remind the hearer that creation is both subject to the curse of sin and the cure. Those that represent believers offer glimpses of restoration despite the less-than-ideal circumstances of the present.[10]

Who Is the Bad Guy?

Given that apocalyptic literature is a special kind of narrative, and that the prophet is the protagonist while God is the hero, who is the villain? Not all visions include an antagonist proper. There are a variety of antagonists in these visions, and knowing who they are drastically affects the focus of sermons on them. We find Satan, pagan earthly kingdoms, those who persecute the church, and idolatrous people within the believing community all as antagonists in apocalyptic visions.

In Revelation 12–13 the clear antagonist is Satan, depicted as a red dragon and "that ancient serpent." He is also the villain in Revelation 20. As Andrew Naselli explains: "A serpent has two major strategies: *deceive* and *devour*. As a general rule, the form a serpent takes depends on its strategy. When a serpent in Scripture attempts to deceive it's a snake. When a serpent attempts to devour, it's a dragon."[11] The key character elements of Satan in these visions is his hostility towards the church and his deception of humanity. He must be and is defeated by God in the end. The fact that Satan is the author of evil is a reminder that, in one sense, when we suffer, we are feeling the consequences of Satan's rebellion against God. The main application thrust in these sermons would be focusing on Satan as the source of sin and suffering and God as the ultimate rescuer.

---

10 We will look more closely at the dynamic of symbols in apocalyptic visions in Chapter 4. With regard to characterization the key observation is to see what the characters represent, not merely what they are in the vision.

11 Andrew David Naselli, *The Serpent and the Serpent Slayer* (Crossway, 2020), 18, emphasis his.

In Daniel's first, second, and fourth visions pagan earthly kingdoms and kings are the villains. In these visions they are represented as beasts, a goat or its horns, a ram, and as kings. In Revelation 17–18 Babylon is the antagonist. G.K. Beale identifies Babylon as "the prevailing economic-religious system in alliance with the state and its related authorities and existing throughout the ages."[12] In these visions the focus is on the defeat of cultural evil, especially as the church suffers as a minority in such cultures.

In Revelation 11 those who persecute the church are the enemies of God and God's people. Their judgment is revealed to give Christians hope in the midst of varying degrees of persecution in the Roman Empire in the first century. Zechariah's second vision also focuses on the nations who attacked God's people. Sermons on these visions should foster perseverance despite opposition to the gospel. Rather than revel in the judgment of the wicked, these passages call for a worshipful sobriety as God vindicates the faith of the church.

The final group of antagonists we find in apocalyptic visions are idolators and those who compromise within the church. These villains show up in Ezekiel's second vision as well as Revelation 14:9–12. This means it is entirely possible that the hearers of the vision themselves would be painted as villains. Confronting hypocrisy and compromise in the community of believers is an important function of apocalyptic visions, however uncomfortable it is. For example, Ezekiel's progressive tour of idolatry in Ezekiel 8 is meant to sicken the hearers at the audacity of such sin, and convict those who are guilty of it.

Homiletical Strategy 3: Invite Hearers to Journey with the Prophet

In light of the cast of characters involved in apocalyptic visions, sermons on apocalyptic can invite hearers to journey with the

---

12 G.K. Beale, *The Book of Revelation,* NIGTC (Eerdmans, 1999), 850. Some dispensational commentators like Robert L. Thomas argue that the reference is to a new kingdom in Babylon during the end times, but even so the significance of what she represents is sinful rebellion against God. See Robert L. Thomas, *Revelation 8–22* (Moody, 1995), 207.

prophet and thus get to know the other characters. Immersing hearers in the world of the prophet as he received the vision will bring these characters to life. Invite hearers on the prophetic journey by helping the modern audience to emotionally connect with the prophet, instilling confidence in God in the sermon, emphasizing the shock value of the characters and imagery, fostering perseverance despite opposition to the gospel, and confronting sin with pastoral care and sensitivity.

Connect the Audience with the Prophet

Inviting hearers to journey with the prophet means helping the modern audience to connect emotionally with the prophet at some level. Shimon Bar-Efrat explains how knowing the characters fosters an emotional connection with the reader/hearer. He explains that characters "generally arouse considerable emotional involvement; we feel what they feel, rejoice in their gladness, grieve at their sorrow and participate in their fate and experiences."[13] Helping the audience to emotionally connect to the prophet means taking time to introduce them to his background and offering specific points of connection along the way. For example, consider this introduction to Daniel from a sermon on Daniel 8:

> You remember Daniel—the teenager forcibly taken from his family and home to a strange new world. He was faced with learning a new language in a new culture complete with strange food and strange gods. You remember his famous stand against idolatry when he wouldn't eat the king's meat, and later as an adult as he survived the lions' den. His remarkable faith made him a light in dark times. In many ways we're facing dark times. We have not been forced to move into spiritual exile, but here we are nonetheless, strangers in our own land. Daniel's generation needed a vision of hope to sustain them through the political ups and downs they and their children and grandchildren would face. Today I can't help but think that we need this same

---

13 Shimon Bar-Efrat, *Narrative Art in the Bible* (T&T Clark International, 2004), 47.

vision. How can we walk by faith in the midst of political turmoil and uncertainty? Let's walk with Daniel today; see what he saw, hear what he heard, and learn what we need to learn to walk by faith.

In a longer sermon series through a book of the Bible you may be able to build a sustained connection between the congregation and the prophet over several sermons. The idea is to take what might be a recognized yet unfamiliar biblical prophet like Zechariah or Ezekiel, and to allow the audience to get to know him and his story. In a one-time sermon context, it will take more time to establish the connection, but it is worth it. We should never assume that hearers are up to speed on the historical circumstances of the prophets in apocalyptic visions.

Another possible means of inviting people to travel with the prophet by identifying with him would be to introduce him and his back story before the sermon in a video or live preview announcement. The benefit of using time outside the sermon to aid in this process is that you will save precious minutes in the sermon itself. In ministry contexts where you have access to people with creative gifts, invite them to use those gifts in helping get the congregation excited about walking with a prophet like Ezekiel.

Instill Confidence in God

Another way characterization in apocalyptic shapes sermons is instilling confidence in hearers by displaying the trustworthiness of the mediator and God the hero. Two aspects of apocalyptic characterization help us here. First, the heavenly mediator reveals that the message of the vision is sent by God. Given that everyone faces uncertainty in so many aspects of life, these passages can have a stabilizing effect. After all, God did send the heavenly mediator.

How can the preacher instill confidence? Tone and body language in delivery are two effective ways of inspiring confidence in the congregation. When it comes to the divinely sanctioned vision explanation the sermon's tone should be clear. Consider speaking somewhat more loudly than usual. These parts of the message should be delivered standing tall, not with shoulders shrugged due to uncertainty. Perhaps even remind hearers that these are the very words of God. Use adjectives and nouns that call to mind strength; use illustrations that foster the concept of confidence.

Second, God being the true hero of these visions should give hearers sure hope. As with the heavenly mediator, the purpose of God revealing his saving work is to instill confidence. While apocalyptic visions bring up many questions we cannot answer, a sermon on an apocalyptic vision should never leave the congregation in a fog of uncertainty. Point people to the ways the vision reveals God as the basis for hope and confidence. Choosing words that reflect the sure hope of God's judging and saving work will help the audience share that hope.

Notice how Ron O'Grady instilled confidence through his word choice and illustrations in this sermon on Revelation 5:

> A strong angel steps forward (v. 2) and asks whether there is someone worthy to open the scroll but there is nobody able to do so. Not Billy Graham or Pope John Paul. Not the World Council of Churches or the Little River Church of God… "I saw… a Lamb standing as if it had been slaughtered…" Slowly the lamb moves forward and takes the scroll from the hand of God (v. 7). All over heaven there is a sigh of relief and the saints of the ages shout with happiness that the lamb has succeeded when all others have failed.[14]

He contrasts faulty sources of hope and confidence with the eternal source of confidence. The strong angel identifies the need, and the Lamb fulfills that need. He highlights the relief and joy in heaven as a result of the Lamb's work. Even in a context of judgment, believers can be inspired to trust God more.

Sermons on apocalyptic visions foster hope in God when they clearly point to God as the only rescuer. Be mindful of not leaving the congregation in a pit of despair regarding current trials

---

14 Ron O'Grady, "The Strength of Weakness," in *Preaching Through the Apocalypse,* ed. Cornish R. Rogers and Joseph R. Jeter Jr. (Chalice, 1992), 84–85.

and sufferings. To miss God as the hero of apocalyptic visions is to leave people without concrete hope. Even in visions where angelic activity is in view, make it clear that these angels are doing the will of God both in judgment and salvation.

Emphasize Shocking Characters

In addition to connecting the audience with the prophet and instilling confidence in God, sermons on apocalyptic visions need to emphasize the shock value of the characters and imagery. Arthurs highlights several ways to maintain the grand scale and extraordinary nature of these visions: "One way to re-create the panoramic quality of visionary literature is with panoramic illustrations."[15] He also suggests "using a slightly elevated style."[16] The idea is to convey the scale of the vision by approximation in the sermon delivery. The use of media support may be helpful here to aid in the homiletic shock and awe campaign. However, be sure that the media is helpful and not merely distracting. If a visual aid is low quality, it will do more harm than good. Sermon delivery on apocalyptic visions should never be dull or boring. In this regard Arthurs also reminds us to use a high level of energy that is a genuine reflection of excitement about the passage.[17]

Call the Audience to Perseverance

Antagonists in apocalyptic visions create the need for a clear call to perseverance in sermons on apocalyptic. The different kinds of antagonists require careful attention. When it comes to visions that reveal Satan, be aware that most of what many think about Satan is informed more by Hollywood than by the Bible. Consider providing a brief summary of his role throughout the Bible.[18] The effect on the audience should be one of relief to know Satan's end

---

15 Arthurs, *Preaching with Variety*, 194.
16 Ibid.
17 Ibid., 195.
18 See Naselli, *The Serpent and the Serpent Slayer*, for a short, insightful biblical summary of Satan's depiction as a serpent in the Bible.

is sure in spite of his attempts to destroy the church and urgency to persevere in light of his opposition. From time to time pull back the curtain and remind people that Satan is destined to lose; his defeat is only a matter of time.

For example, in a sermon on Revelation 12 consider referencing other passages that underline Satan's defeat while calling the audience to persevere:

> As we see in passages like 2 Corinthians 10:3–6 and Ephesians 6:10–20, Satan attacks our faith, our beliefs, and our worldview. He wants us to refuse to believe that he exists, and that he is raging. But the vision reveals Satan exists, and while he is a finite being, he and his demons are on the offensive all around us, raging against God's church. Our victory over Satan by the Lamb means his rage is in vain. We may suffer his attacks, but he cannot defeat us. We may even die, but because of the Lamb we are still victorious. Therefore, we as the Church need to be ready to endure Satan's attacks.

Furthermore, when preaching on visions where the unbelieving majority culture is the antagonist, be sure to identify ways the current church exists as a minority. The big picture here is that evil will not prevail; God will judge all evil.[19] Be careful to nuance these sermons in light of the complementary reality of God's love for the lost. When preaching these visions, we should present a sober assessment of the need for perseverance in the midst of an unbelieving culture with a tenderness and love for the lost. Note that perseverance is necessary because of the many ways evil is expressed in a culture.

Confront with Care

Finally, in some visions the antagonists are compromising Christians in the church and therefore the preacher needs to confront this sin directly. When preaching on these visions be careful to apply them with an appropriate level of confrontation and sensitivity

---

[19] We will revisit this theme in Chapter 5.

to the audience. A tone of urgency and warning would fit these visions well. Consider using illustrations that communicate the severity of sin. Bold statements of confrontation are appropriate here, but watch out that the audience does not feel attacked. The vision is given as a helpful rebuke from a loving shepherd, not an assault from an enemy.

Summary of Homiletical Strategy 3

Inviting hearers to journey with the prophet means engaging the congregation's imagination. The sermon's tone, structure, and focus should allow the audience to feel the circumstances and topic of the vision. The preacher can accomplish this by:

- helping the modern audience to emotionally connect with the prophet,
- instilling confidence in God,
- emphasizing the shock value of the characters and imagery,
- fostering perseverance in spite of opposition to the gospel,
- applying confrontation with pastoral care and sensitivity.

So far we have considered two ways to following the narrative contours of apocalyptic visions: narrative plot awareness and attention to the characters in the vision. But catching and casting the vision not only requires identifying the basic literary structure of the vision, it also requires listening for the aural effects of apocalyptic visions—the subject of Chapter Three.

For Further Study

Arthurs, Jeffrey. *Preaching with Variety.* Kregel Academic, 2007. Note especially the chapters on apocalyptic and narrative (62–101, 178–199).

Ryken, Leland. *How to Read the Bible as Literature.* Zondervan, 1984. Focus on his chapter on visionary literature (164–175).

Talk about It

What are the specific challenges in dealing with the different kinds of antagonists in apocalyptic visions? Which will be most difficult for you? Why?

Discuss the spiritual benefit of engaging the congregation's imagination during a sermon.

Dig Deeper

Review the chapter on visions in Leland Ryken's book *How to Read the Bible as Literature* (164–175). Take note of the similarities and differences between historical narrative and the first-person vision reports of apocalyptic.

Practice

Identify the characters in Zechariah 5:1–4. Who would you identify as the antagonist? Is God the hero of this vision? Explain your answer. How would you apply it to a contemporary audience? Flesh out some of the ways you would invite the congregation to journey with the prophet in this particular vision.

3

Aural Effects of Apocalyptic: The Sound of the Vision

> ...the Apocalypse of St. John is a majestic image of a high and stately tragedy, shutting and intermingling her solemn scenes and acts with a sevenfold chorus of hallelujahs and harping symphonies.[1]
>
> John Milton

MILTON'S OBSERVATION ABOUT REVELATION also applies to the entire genre of apocalyptic literature. Apocalyptic visions are majestic images that spur us on to imagine not only remarkable sights but also sounds. These visions are well known for their visual elements, but they also have an aural effect: they were read and heard. Preaching apocalyptic demands giving attention to how the visions communicate, including how they were heard. When crafting sermons on apocalyptic we need to listen for the aural effect.

Since the mid-20th century biblical scholars have grown more aware of the aural aspects of biblical texts. (The term "aural" refers to what someone hears.[2]) David Seal reminds us that the original recipients of biblical literature heard the text rather than read it: "For the ancient cultures of the biblical world, hearing was the

---

[1] John Milton, "The Reason of Church Government Urged Against Prelaty," *The Prose Works of John Milton* (George Bell and Sons, 1875), 2:479.

[2] David Seal, "Sensitivity to Aural Elements of a Text: Some Acoustical Elements in Revelation," *Journal of Biblical and Pneumatological Research* 3 (2011): 38 note 3.

primary mode of knowing and experiencing."[3] This means that biblical literature was composed with an awareness by the author that their text would be heard as well as read. Interpretation of biblical texts should accordingly take into account the aural component of how a text sounds when it is read aloud.

Fred Craddock argued that preaching is an oral and aural event and not a literary event: "...preaching is by its nature an acoustical event, having its home in orality not textuality."[4] Incorporating the aural effect of biblical apocalyptic into a sermon is not only feasible, it is an ideal way to allow the form of the genre to impact the sermon.

Interpretive Insights

Aural effects are poetic figures of speech specifically defined by an auditory response in the hearers. Wilfred Watson's *Classical Hebrew Poetry* is a standard handbook for Hebrew poetic devices. Notice how he links specific Hebrew poetic devices to pronunciation: "When considering poetic devices involving sound—assonance, alliteration, rhyme, onomatopoeia, and wordplay—the pronunciation of a language is very much to the fore."[5] How words are spoken and heard are the basis of certain poetic techniques.

Since biblical apocalyptic is narrative, we do not find poetic structures as in the Psalms or OT wisdom literature. Robert Alter observed that apocalyptic vision reports are naturally suited to prose: "One common type of prophecy for which prose seems to have been preferred is the oracular vision, like those that take up a good part of Zechariah...."[6] For example, in OT apocalyptic texts we do not find clausal parallelism, the classic hallmark of Hebrew poetry.

---

3 Ibid., 38.

4 Fred B. Craddock, *Preaching* (Abingdon, 1985), 31. The term "orality" refers to the spoken effect on the giving end, whereas "aural" refers to how such effects are heard on the receiving end.

5 Wilfred G.E. Watson, *Classical Hebrew Poetry: A Guide to its Techniques.* JSOTSup 26 (JSOT Press, 1984), 222.

6 Robert Alter, *The Art of Biblical Poetry,* rev. and updated ed. (Basic Books, 2011), 172.

Even so, as a special kind of prophetic narrative, biblical apocalyptic texts exhibit many features also present in poetry. When it comes to aural effects in biblical apocalyptic literature, we find Watson's list of five techniques present in both Hebrew and Greek apocalyptic texts: alliteration, assonance, rhyme, onomatopoeia, and wordplay. Each of these poetic tools is used with a specific rhetorical purpose or function in view. In some cases, these features are used in exalted prose, while in others small outbursts of poetry occur within a vision. When we see these techniques in an apocalyptic text, we need to ask what the aural effect on the audience was.[7]

Alliteration

Alliteration is the repetition of the same consonant "within a unit of verse."[8] It is worth noting that alliteration need not be limited to the first letter of a word. In short, it is the repetition of consonants for aural effect.

According to Watson, the function of alliteration is cohesion: "The principal function of alliteration is cohesive in nature...."[9] Seal points out that it serves as a mnemonic aid in several ways: "... alliteration can focus a listener's attention, give a sense of energetic imperative, and signal the end to a section of writing."[10]

Assonance

Assonance is to vowels what alliteration is to consonants. Watson clarifies: "It occurs when there is a series of words containing a distinctive vowel-sound or certain vowel-sounds in a specific sequence."[11] Think of assonance as vowel sound repetition. An example in English would be "Fly a kite." Note the long vowel in both fly and kite.

---

7 Discerning aural effects in biblical apocalyptic texts requires basic proficiency in biblical languages. Commentaries on the Hebrew or Greek text should bring such features to light.
8 Watson, *Classical Hebrew Poetry*, 225.
9 Ibid., 227.
10 Seal, "Sensitivity," 44.
11 Watson, *Classical Hebrew Poetry*, 223.

Assonance is all about intensity and emotion. Paul Saydon notes that assonance "is intended as a means of expressing emphasis."[12] The aural effect of assonance is emotional. Saydon identifies three ways assonance expresses intensity of emotion: stressing the meaning of a word through vowel emphasis, repeating a word for emphasis, using two synonymous terms with similar vowels.[13] "Intensity of expression is best reproduced by the stress laid on a word or on one of its constituent elements. Therefore, the most natural way of expressing emphasis is by strengthening or prolonging the pronunciation of a word...."[14] Functionally, assonance is often connected with onomatopoeia (see below) as it "helps link sound with meaning."[15]

Rhyme

For many the most easily recognizable aural feature in apocalyptic is rhyme. Watson states that in rhyme the corresponding sounds need not be exact: "This sound-identity can be of varying degrees, from almost perfect to merely approximate, so that the corresponding rhyme will be within the range of good to near-rhyme."[16] While rhyme is the primary poetic technique for poetry in English, it is not as prominent as a poetic device in Biblical Hebrew and Greek. Often instances of rhyme are better analyzed as assonance or alliteration.

Similar to alliteration and assonance, rhyme is used to provide structure.[17] Think of rhyme as acoustic bullet points. Rhyme provides cohesion and a sense of unity to words, phrases, or clauses. This cohesion results in emphasis of similarities or differences in the groups.

---

12 Paul P. Saydon, "Assonance in Hebrew as a means of expressing emphasis," *Biblica* 36 (1955): 37.

13 Ibid., 37–38. He adds a fourth which is a variation on using two different but synonymous terms.

14 Ibid.

15 Watson, *Classical Hebrew Poetry*, 224.

16 Ibid., 229.

17 Ibid., 233.

Onomatopoeia

Onomatopoeia is "when the pronunciation of a word or a combination of words creates a sound which seems to closely resemble the sound it denotes."[18] It is not an attempt to recreate the sound exactly, but rather is "the imitation of a sound within the rules of the language concerned."[19] Thus in English terms like "roar" or "buzz" are grammatical forms that also imitate the sound to which they refer. Onomatopoeia is a phenomenon in every language, even though different languages approximate different sounds in different ways.

Onomatopoeia adds vividness to a text. Seal argues that the idea is to bring words to life for the hearer: "The main purpose of sound imitation is to enhance the imagery of the scene, thereby giving substance to bare words."[20] This scene enhancement also heightens the emotional element of the text.

Wordplay

Wordplay is based on root similarity and ambiguity in meaning. Watson lists seven distinct forms of Hebrew wordplay, but for our purposes we will focus on turn and polysemantic pun. Turn refers to the repetition of a root (or homonymous roots) with or without a variation in meaning (think of the use of אשר (*asher*) in Psalm 1:1 to mean both "blessed" and as a relative pronoun). The repetition creates the aural effect. Polysemantic pun is the use of a root with a potential double meaning. Watson notes that this use is rare.[21] One such occurrence may be in Revelation 1:18 where the title ὁ ζῶν is used for Jesus. David Aune argues that here the term is used "as a double entendre referring both to a traditional Jewish designation for God and to the triumph of Jesus over death through his resurrection."[22]

---

18 Seal, "Sensitivity," 44.
19 Watson, *Classical Hebrew Poetry*, 234.
20 Seal, "Sensitivity," 44.
21 Watson, *Classical Hebrew Poetry*, 242.
22 David A. Aune, *Revelation 1–5*, WBC 52a (Zondervan, 1997), 102.

Wordplay can be used for a variety of functions. Authors use it to create and sustain amusement, to denote a reversal of fortune, to equate two people or things, or as an explanation of a proper noun.[23] Most uses of wordplay involve comparison. Discerning wordplay requires in-depth knowledge of the original languages, but thorough critical commentaries should draw attention to them. Compared to other aural effects, wordplay is relatively rare in biblical apocalyptic literature.

Homiletical Strategy 4: Echo the Aural Effect

After identifying an aural effect and its function in an apocalyptic text, the task remains to echo it in the sermon. Focusing on the aural effect in a sermon has experiential benefits for the hearers. Michael Williams suggests that one performative benefit of homiletic awareness of aural effects is added vividness: "An oral/aural homiletic would encourage a vividness and concreteness in language that can create moments of doing and happening in the pulpit. Here is a reaffirmation of the incarnate quality of the spoken word, that it takes on the immediacy of lived experience."[24] Additionally, aural effects awaken the imagination. Williams describes how spoken words welcome the hearers to a new world: "Words spoken in all their vividness and concreteness create an imaginal world for the listener and invite those who hear into that world. This is why the spoken word emerges in imagery and story, poetry and song so often."[25]

Echoing the aural effect can be accomplished in several ways. First, echo the aural effect by recreating the effect of the biblical text in the language of the sermon. For example, if alliteration is used in the text, the preacher would seek comparable terms that also achieve alliteration. While this might seem to be the most attractive option for echoing the aural effect, in practice it is very

---

23 Watson, *Classical Hebrew Poetry*, 245–246; Valérie Kabergs and Hans Ausloos, "Paronomasia or wordplay? A Babel-Like Confusion: Towards a Definition of Hebrew Wordplay," *Biblica* 93.1 (2012): 18–19.

24 Michael E. Williams, "Toward an Oral/Aural Homiletic," *Homiletic* 11 (1986): 3.

25 Ibid.

difficult due to linguistic and semantic differences between the biblical text and other languages. A second means of echoing the aural effect is to target the function. If the function of alliteration in the text is to focus attention, the preacher can use another aural effect that accomplishes the same effect. If neither of those strategies is effective, a third means of echoing the aural effect would be to explain it to the audience and perhaps even read it in the original so that they can hear it. The main drawback of this strategy is that it merely explains the effect without allowing the hearers to truly experience it. As we consider the five poetic techniques that result in aural effects, we will highlight some biblical cases and explore some examples of how to echo the effect in a sermon.

Use an Equivalent to Alliteration

Alliteration often lends itself well to using an equivalent. One example of alliteration in biblical apocalyptic is in Revelation 4:11, where John hears the 24 elders singing praise to God. The first line in English reads: "Our Lord and God, you are worthy to receive glory and honor and power." In Greek we see alliteration with the dental consonants τ and δ (*t* and *d*) in the three objects of the verb "receive," ἄξιος εἶ, ὁ κύριος καὶ ὁ θεὸς ἡμῶν, λαβεῖν *τὴν δόξαν* καὶ *τὴν τιμὴν* καὶ *τὴν δύναμιν* ("worthy are you, O Lord our God, to receive the glory and the honor and the power").[26]

In this case alliteration focuses the hearers' attention on the three attributes of God mentioned. The main idea of the clause is God being worthy of praise for his glory, honor, and power. The alliteration has an aural effect of acoustically underlining those particular reasons for praising God. If this expression of praise is a song, then the alliteration may also serve as a mnemonic aide.

Echoing this effect could be accomplished via a functional equivalent. In English one aural effect that focuses attention is to pause between words or phrases. In this case consider reading Revelation 4:11 with extra breaks between the objects of the verb receive, "Our Lord and God, you are worthy to receive glory [PAUSE] and honor [PAUSE] and power."

---

26 Emphasis mine.

Daniel 9:24 provides another example of alliteration in biblical apocalyptic literature. In this vision the angel Gabriel is explaining the 70 weeks of years to the prophet Daniel. Gabriel says:

> Seventy weeks are decreed about your people and your holy city—to bring the rebellion to an end, to put a stop to sin, to atone for iniquity, to bring in everlasting righteousness, to seal up vision and prophecy, and to anoint the most holy place.

In this case the verb "decree" has six verbal complements that are infinitives. In Hebrew those infinitives are all marked by a prefixed לְ (*l*). The aural effect of the repetition of the consonant לְ (*l*) focuses the hearer's attention on the purposes of the 70 weeks and emphasizes the unity and completeness of the list.

Echoing the alliteration in Daniel 9:24 in a sermon can be accomplished by recreating the exact same aural effect. English translations have already accomplished this by using the word "to" in front of the verbs to mark them as infinitives, "…to bring … to an end, to put a stop…, to atone…, to bring in…, to seal up…, and to anoint…." In a sermon you might highlight the effect by intentionally pausing between phrases as you read the text in order to create aural symmetry.

Recreate or Explain Assonance

In apocalyptic texts we find examples of assonance that add emphasis and intensity of emotion. In Ezekiel 9:4 the prophet Ezekiel witnesses the Lord command a scribe to identify repentant people in Jerusalem: "'Pass throughout the city of Jerusalem,' the Lord said to him, 'and put a mark on the foreheads of the men who sigh and groan over all the detestable practices committed in it.'" In this statement the phrase "the men who sigh and groan" is a translation of הָאֲנָשִׁים הַנֶּאֱנָחִים וְהַנֶּאֱנָקִים. Daniel Block highlights the extremely strong assonance in this phrase, particularly between the last two words: "The translation moan and groan attempts to preserve the rhyme and assonance of *hā'ănāšîm hanne'ĕnāḥîm wĕhanne'ĕnāqîm*."[27] Contextually, this sighing is an emotional response of the faithful to the sin of idolatry. Block again clarifies: "Here the scribe is to search for individuals who will display a similar emotion over all the abominations (*tô'ēbôt*) being perpetrated in Jerusalem...."[28]

The translators of the NIV were able to echo the aural effect of the assonance in Ezekiel 9:4 by their translation "moan and groan." A preacher who is using a different translation can highlight the assonance by substituting "moan and groan" for alternative translations. The preacher can further echo the effect by lengthening the vowels, "mooaan and grooaan" in reading or explaining the verse. Another option for echoing this aural effect would be to aim for the same functional effect. In this instance the effect is emphasizing emotional disgust over idolatry. In English terms of disgust like "ugh" or "ewww" would accomplish the same aural effect conveying emotional dismay.

Revelation 10:3 contains another example of assonance in apocalyptic literature. In this part of John's vision an angel with a little scroll descends from heaven. He stood on sea and land "and he called out with a loud voice like a roaring lion. When he cried out, the seven thunders raised their voices." Seal observes that in the Greek of the first clause (καὶ ἔκραξεν φωνῇ μεγάλῃ ὥσπερ λέων μυκᾶται) "the plethora of open mouth vowels in the sentence helps convey the volume of the scream. Consequently, the listeners hear the loud ominous cry of pending judgment."[29]

Echoing this instance of assonance can be accomplished through recreating the effect. In English the participle "roaring" easily allows for emphasizing the vowels. In addition, mirroring the effect of a loud cry can also be accomplished through the preacher raising the volume of their voice. In this case both methods can be used simultaneously. The impending judgment of God is the reason for this emotional cry. As an alternative way to achieve the same effect the preacher could use the illustration of a bailiff

---

27 Daniel I. Block, *The Book of Ezekiel Chapters 1–24*, NICOT (Eerdmans, 1997), 307.

28 Ibid.

29 Seal, "Sensitivity," 47.

shouting "All rise!" as a judge enters the courtroom. This illustration conveys a similar sense of sobriety in a judgement context.

Reproduce the Effect of Rhyme

Directly echoing the aural effect of rhyme is not possible in most cases. However, the preacher can reproduce the effect. In Revelation 5:12 the apostle John hears the worship of the Lamb in heaven. The countless multitude said: "Worthy is the Lamb who was slaughtered to receive power and riches and wisdom and strength and honor and glory and blessing!" Seal makes the observation that John "strings together thirteen terms all ending in *n*, thereby creating a strong rhythmical cadence to the song."[30] These terms also rhyme or near-rhyme. The aural effect emphasizes the unity and totality of this list of reasons to praise the Lamb. It also adds intensity as the list continues on.

In this case the preacher can use different means of emphasizing a long list with escalating intensity. As we saw previously with alliteration, the use of dramatic pause between items in a list draws attention to each item: "Worthy is the Lamb who was slaughtered to receive power [PAUSE], and riches [PAUSE]...." Alternatively, preachers can emphasize the cumulative weight of a long list by reading the list quickly and then pausing at the end of the list. This technique allows hearers to be impacted by the totality of the list, while also giving them a few seconds to reflect on it.

Recreate the Effect of Onomatopoeia

In a few rare cases, onomatopoeia in a biblical text can be directly recreated. In Zechariah 2:13 the prophet is recounting his third night vision. This vision details the glorious future of Jerusalem as the city where God will dwell with his people without threat of foreign invaders. He also hears of the judgment God will pronounce and enact upon those who have been his enemies. In Zechariah 2:13 the angelic mediator calls for a worshipful silence in response to the judgment and salvation of God: "Let all people be silent

---

30 Ibid., 48.

before the Lord, for from his holy dwelling he has roused himself." In Hebrew the interjection הַס (*has*) functions as the imperative "be silent."[31] This interjection sounds like the English interjection "Hush." In this case the onomatopoeia is that the word sounds like the silence or quiet it calls for. In Zechariah 2:13 this interjection heightens the emotional element in the vision. In response to the judging and saving work of God the entire earth is summoned to be silent before him.

The preacher can directly echo this example of onomatopoeia by using the English equivalent "hush."[32] The aural effect can be heightened by elongating the pronunciation and allowing for silence after the word. Another technique to create the heightened emotion of silence would be to pronounce the term loudly with a sudden stop. The key effect here is that the audience would have space to be impacted by the force of God's holiness as revealed in the text. Allowing for times of silence in a sermon is difficult for many preachers, but it is essential in some cases as we seek to recreate the aural effect.

As with rhyme, in most cases the best homiletic strategy for echoing onomatopoeia is to recreate the effect using a different technique. In Revelation 8:13 John sees and hears an eagle crying out to the inhabitants of the earth: "I looked and heard an eagle flying high overhead, crying out in a loud voice, 'Woe! Woe! Woe to those who live on the earth, because of the remaining trumpet blasts that the three angels are about to sound!'" The term "woe" is onomatopoetic as it resembles the cry of the eagle, and it is repeated three times for emphasis (οὐαὶ οὐαὶ οὐαὶ). G.K. Beale points out the dire imagery in use here: "The picture in Rev. 8:13 is of an eagle hovering over its prey."[33] The onomatopoeic term adds audio to the visual: "This warning is enhanced by the shrill cry of the bird...."[34] Thus the emotion heightened by the eagle's cry is fear and sobriety in light of God's judgment.

---

31 HALOT, 253.

32 See the translation in Ralph L. Smith, *Micah-Malachi*, WBC 32 (Zondervan, 1984), 194–195.

33 G.K. Beale, *The Book of Revelation*, NIGTC (Eerdmans, 1999), 490.

34 Seal, "Sensitivity," 46.

In order to recreate the aural effect of this instance of onomatopoeia, the preacher needs to guide the audience to feel the same sobriety and reverential fear in response to the judgment of God. In this case mirroring the function with another technique is likely the most effective strategy. One option would be to use a quiet tone of voice and a slow rate of speech: "Woe... woe... woe...." This tone communicates the seriousness of the situation, especially when combined with the visual of an eagle circling its prey.

Explain the Aural Effect of Wordplay

In the case of wordplay, the only technique to recreate the effect in the sermon is to explain the aural effect. While this is admittedly the least effective way to echo an aural effect, it is better than ignoring it entirely. In Daniel 8 the prophet Daniel is given the vision of the goat and the ram. In verse 15, after he was given the initial vision, he saw the angel Gabriel and described him as "someone who appeared to be a man." In verse 16 we find out this one's name is Gabriel. Andrew Hill explains the wordplay: "Commentators acknowledge the clear wordplay between the phrase for the figure who 'looks like a man' (Heb. כְּמַרְאֵה־גָבֶר) and the name 'Gabriel' (Heb. גַּבְרִיאֵל)."[35] Here the wordplay serves to draw attention to the contrast between Daniel, a mere man, and the angel Gabriel. This explains the reason why Daniel falls down in terror in Daniel 8:17.

In this instance the preacher might briefly point out the wordplay and highlight its significance:

> There is a play on words with the phrase 'one who looks like a man' and the name Gabriel... Gabriel can mean man of God or God is my hero. Gabriel is an angel and is definitely not a man. This explains why Daniel was so overcome and collapsed in verse 17. It's also a good reminder that although scary things will happen, even God's servants are far more powerful than we can fathom.

---

35 Andrew E. Hill, *Daniel-Malachi,* Expositor's Bible Commentary (Zondervan, 2004), 152.

Non-Aural Techniques

As we have seen, in some cases recreating the aural effect of apocalyptic is not possible through aural means. For those times consider using other methods like varying intonation or using physical gestures. In many OT apocalyptic visions the prophet introduces the next part of the vision by using the emphatic particle הִנֵּה (*hinneh*), often translated "Look!" or "Behold!" Zechariah uses this dramatic device regularly in his night visions. For example, in Zechariah 2:1 he writes: "Then I lifted my eyes and I looked, and behold—four horns!"[36] In preaching this sermon an effective way to capture the aural effect by non-aural means is to point somewhere in the room and read the text in a tone of urgency, then convey the reason why the four horns were shocking or important. The idea is to recreate the surprise of the original and communicate the reason.

Summary of Homiletical Strategy 4

Although apocalyptic is not poetry, it makes use of certain poetic features to create aural effects. As we craft sermons on these passages, we should seek to echo the aural effects by direct mirroring of the technique, seeking a functional equivalent, or explaining the aural effect. The goal in echoing aural effects is to allow hearers to feel and experience these visions.

1. Use a functional equivalent to echo alliteration.
2. Recreate or explain assonance.
3. Reproduce the effect of rhyme.
4. Recreate the effect of onomatopoeia.
5. Explain the aural effect of wordplay.

In our progress preparing sermons on apocalyptic we have learned to identify the narrative structure and characters and to listen for the aural effects of the vision. Our next challenge in catching and casting the vision is to confront the imposing feature of figurative language in apocalyptic visions.

---

36 Translation mine.

For Further Study

Alter, Robert. *The Art of Biblical Poetry.* Rev. ed. (Basic Books, 2011).

Watson, Wilfred G.E. *Classical Hebrew Poetry: A Guide to its Techniques.* JSOTSup 26 (JSOT Press, 1984), 222–250.

Talk about It

What are reasons an author might incorporate poetic techniques in a non-poetic text? What will people miss if we ignore the aural effects of a passage?

Dig Deeper

Familiarize yourself with Watson's explanation and analysis of sound use in Hebrew poetry. Compare and contrast preaching an apocalyptic text versus preaching a poetic text.

Practice

Look for aural effects in Revelation 12:1–12. As you identify them, consider how they are functioning in the passage. How do they enhance the vision report and engage the imagination? Finally, practice echoing the aural effects using one of the techniques described in this chapter.

4

Apocalyptic Figurative Language: Signs, Symbols, and Numbers

> *If the seer of the vision asked for an interpretation, much more may you and I. He was not idly curious, but reverently teachable; let us imitate his holy diligence in desiring to learn.*[1]
> —C.H. Spurgeon

As we endeavor to preach the apocalyptic visions of the Bible we would be wise to make use of built-in guides. Our guides come in the form of visual symbols and heavenly vision mediators—two norms of apocalyptic literature. In these visions the use of signs, symbols, and numbers is often frustrating and controversial. But these guides are meant to clarify—not obscure—the meaning of the vision. Rather than fear the symbolic nature of apocalyptic, we need to let the guides do their job.

Visions necessarily include signs and referents—key watermarks of apocalyptic literature. Frederick Murphy notes that apocalyptic language is "both literal and metaphorical" and "has allegorical features and concrete referents."[2] Describing the apocalyptic nature of the book of Revelation, Michael Kuykendall explains how its symbolism "also extends to numbers, colors, places, and institutions as well."[3] Allowing the literary features of apocalyptic

---

1 C.H. Spurgeon, "Two Visions," in *Spurgeon's Sermons,* Vol. 10 (Ages Software, 1989), electronic ed.

2 Frederick J. Murphy, *Apocalypticism in the Bible and Its World: A Comprehensive Introduction* (Baker Academic, 2012), 13.

3 Michael Kuykendall, *Lions, Locusts, and the Lamb: Interpreting Key Images in the Book of Revelation* (Wipf & Stock, 2019), 3.

texts to influence sermon crafting requires dealing faithfully with the symbolic nature of visions.

Interpretive Insights

At this point we come across one of the main interpretive questions regarding apocalyptic: are the signs, symbols, and numbers in apocalyptic visions to be interpreted literally or figuratively? How we answer this question has significant implications for eschatology as well as practical theology and homiletics. Key factors to consider here are the nature of signs and their referents, the kinds of signs in apocalyptic visions, and the explanations of the vision mediators.

The Symbolic Nature of Visions: Signs and Referents

In order to appreciate the nature of figurative language, the key terms "sign" (or "symbol") and "referent" must be defined with precision. When describing figurative language in apocalyptic literature, the term "sign" refers to a participant, prop, image, action, or number in the visionary world that symbolically represents a corresponding person, thing, action, or duration of time in real time and space. Norman Perrin notes that the norm in apocalyptic literature is a one-to-one correspondence of sign (or symbol) to referent: "Typically, the apocalyptic seer told the story of the history of his people in symbols where each symbol bore a one-to-one relationship with that which it depicted."[4] Thus, we should expect most apocalyptic signs to stand for a single real-world referent.

Occasionally, signs may have more than one referent, or they may have multiple levels of symbolic layering. Bandy cites the example in Revelation 17:9–10 where the seven heads of the beast are a sign whose referent is simultaneously seven hills and seven kings.[5] In the case of the seven golden lampstands in Revelation 1,

---

4 Norman Perrin, "Eschatology and Hermeneutics: Reflections on Method in the Interpretation of the New Testament," in *Journal of Biblical Literature* 93 (2010): 11.

5 Alan Bandy, "The Hermeneutics of Symbolism: How to Interpret the

the lampstands are a sign representing seven churches. Those seven churches may further be a sign whose referent is the church throughout time. Identifying signs and referents in apocalyptic visions is a fundamental task in preparation for preaching. The sermon cannot explain and apply these symbols without clear analysis of signs and referents in the vision.

For many interpreters the default interpretive position is that visions must be interpreted literally if at all possible. Roy Zuck articulates this view in his chapter on prophecy in *Basic Bible Interpretation*: "Figurative language is present if the statement taken in its normal sense would be impossible or illogical."[6] Robert Thomas also argues for this approach in the introduction to his two-volume commentary on Revelation. He acknowledges the difficulty of prescribing a "literal interpretation" to a book filled with signs: "One may wonder how a book of symbols and visions such as Revelation can be interpreted literally. This is not so difficult to understand if one keeps in mind that the symbols and visions were the means of communicating the message to the prophet, *but they have a literal meaning unless otherwise indicated in the text.*"[7]

For these interpreters to allow for signs in visions to be interpreted figuratively without explicit textual indication would be to allow a hermeneutical free-for-all—any sign could refer to anything an interpreter desired. Charles Ryrie warned, "If one does not use the plain, normal, or literal method of interpretation, all objectivity is lost."[8] Even so, a strictly literal approach to apocalyptic can easily result in faulty sign identification. For example, some have thought it obvious that the description of flying demon locusts in Revelation 9:1–11 was John's way of describing Apache attack helicopters!

The danger of irresponsible interpretation of signs and symbols is avoided by a recognition of the genre itself. The signs, symbols, and numbers in apocalyptic are meant to be read as true in their

---

Symbols of John's Apocalypse," *Southern Baptist Journal of Theology* 14.1 (2010): 49.

6 Roy B. Zuck, *Basic Bible Interpretation* (Chariot Victor, 1991), 244.

7 Robert Thomas, *Revelation 1–7* (Moody, 1992), 35, emphasis mine.

8 Charles C. Ryrie, *Dispensationalism* (Moody, 1995), 29.

literary sense (e.g., the visionary dragon of Revelation 12 refers to Satan, but Satan is not literally a dragon). Allowing the genre of the text to determine the way symbols are interpreted takes the author's intent seriously. Interpret signs and symbols figuratively with literal referents rather than insisting on a literalistic interpretation.[9] An awareness of the literary features of a text yields interpreters who are "sensitive to contexts and familiar with how literary texts work."[10]

Acknowledging the literary genre of apocalyptic visions means "elevating the primacy of the symbolic while wanting to avoid reducing symbols to something totally spiritual...."[11] The preacher should respect the fact that signs, symbols, and even numbers in apocalyptic visions figuratively refer to real-world referents. Thus, to adopt a primarily figurative interpretation of apocalyptic visions is not to abandon a high view of Scripture or the interpretive principle of authorial intent. Even though interpreters with different views of eschatology will disagree on the literal referent of a sign (e.g., what the two witnesses of Revelation 12 represent), they can agree on the highly symbolic nature of apocalyptic literature.

The signs in apocalyptic visions are just that, signs, but they point to literal referents. In many cases the vision mediator reveals the referent for an important sign or symbol. Sometimes the symbol and referent are the same: the leaders of Jerusalem in Zechariah's second vision are the leaders of Jerusalem. Most of the time signs are a symbolic representation that communicates a key characteristic of the referent. In Zechariah's fourth vision the mediator has to explain what the golden lampstand and two olive trees represent: God's Spirit at work (Zech 4:1–7).

Some visionary referents are not clear. If a symbol's referent is less than obvious, a helpful commentary or Bible background resource may come to the rescue. One example is the image of blood in the battle of Armageddon filling the valley up to the chests of the

---

9 For an excellent treatment on the hermeneutics of signs and symbols see Bandy, "The Hermeneutics of Symbolism," 46–58. For a similar step by step approach to interpreting signs see Kuykendall, *Lions, Locusts, and the Lamb*, 7–9.

10 Kevin J. Vanhoozer, *Is There a Meaning in This Text?* (Zondervan, 1998), 311.

11 Bandy, "The Hermeneutics of Symbolism," 49.

horses in Revelation 14:20. Richard Bauckham enlightens us to the fact that the same image is used in non-canonical apocalyptic texts like 1 Enoch 100:3 and 4 Ezra 15:35–36.[12] This known usage of the symbol "clearly shows that Revelation 14:20 makes use of a topos which was widely used to indicate slaughter, in war, of exceptional proportions."[13]

Specific Signs in Apocalyptic

Figurative imagery in apocalyptic includes people, animals, natural elements, props, angelic actions, and spiritually significant numbers. Each category of imagery presents particular challenges to an audience far removed from the original context. Even so, thinking through these categories ahead of time equips the preacher to engage his audience's imagination and help them see, hear, and feel the impact of these visions.[14] After surveying some common signs in biblical apocalyptic we will consider relevant homiletic strategies. First, we need to get to know the signs.

People

People in apocalyptic visions are not always signs; sometimes they are simply themselves (e.g., the prophets who received the visions do not stand as a sign for something else, rather they simply participate in the vision as themselves). When used as a sign people may stand for a larger group, an abstract concept, or even an ideology.

First, individuals may represent a larger group or collective. Interpreters debate the referent of the two witnesses in Revelation 11:1–13. One option is to take them literally and thus conclude they are two individuals.[15] Others, like N.T. Wright, see them as "a symbol for the whole church in its prophetic witness, its faithful

---

12   Richard Bauckham, *The Climax of Prophecy* (T&T Clark, 1993),40.
13   Ibid., 43.
14   The examples in this section are not exhaustive, but rather provide a sample of some significant signs used in canonical apocalyptic literature.
15   E.g., Robert Thomas takes them to be Moses and Elijah. See Thomas, *Revelation 8–22*, 88–89.

death, and its vindication by God."[16] Note that in either interpretation the witnesses in the vision are faithful unto death and are raised from the dead. Thus, they serve as a model of faith in the midst of persecution.

Second, individuals may stand for an abstract concept. For example, in Zechariah's vision in 5:5–11 he sees a woman in a basket. The angelic guide reveals what she represents: "This is wickedness" (Zech 5:8).

Finally, sometimes individuals stand for a particular ideology. In Revelation 17:3–5 a woman in a purple dress sitting on a red beast is a sign representing Babylon. She is later described as "the great city that has royal power over the kings of the earth" (Rev 17:18). Most interpreters understand her as a representation of anti-Christian cultural influence, of which Rome would have been the prime example in the first century. In this case the visual is emphasized—her purple dress and ornate jewelry connote prostitution. The reader is meant to be disgusted by her immorality, and a sermon on this vision should recreate that disgust.

Animals

Animals are frequently used in apocalyptic visions as signs. Sometimes strange beasts are envisioned, and even horns on beasts are used as signs. When preaching these visions, keep in mind the audience will need help focusing on the relevance of the animal for the meaning of the vision. For some sign animals the relevance is obvious, but others will need explaining.

Certain animals were used as signs because of well-known characteristics or physical traits, and often those traits are identifiable in other biblical texts or even non-canonical apocalyptic works. The red dragon of Revelation 12 is also called "that ancient serpent" (Rev 12:9). D.A. Carson notes: "Dragon, leviathan, monster of the deep—these are standard symbols for all that opposes God, and sometimes for the Devil himself."[17] In this case the ser-

---

16 N.T. Wright, *Revelation for Everyone* (Westminster John Knox, 2011), 98. See also Bauckham, *The Climax of Prophecy*, 274.

17 D.A. Carson, *Scandalous: The Cross and Resurrection of Jesus* (Crossway,

pent represents Satan because of the trait of deception; he is Satan, "the one who deceives the whole world" (Rev 12:9). In a sermon on this vision, a quick reminder of the serpent's deceit of Eve in Genesis 3 might be a great way to bring the relevant trait of deception to the minds of listeners.

Animals often represent nations in apocalyptic visions. In the vision of Daniel 8 a ram and goat represent Medo-Persia and Greece, respectively. The ram is chosen because of its natural power. Andrew Hill notes: "The ram's power is irresistible, and it charges at will in three directions...."[18] Likewise the goat shows speed and agility: "The goat appears suddenly from the west and is notable for its swift movement...."[19]

In Daniel 8 we also find an example of horns on the ram and goat being used as signs. Carson reminds us that "Horns typically signify kings or king-dominion: awesome power and kingly authority."[20] Murphy confirms this association: "Animal horns are frequent symbols for strength in the Bible, often in a military context. In apocalyptic symbolism, they often represent kings or royal strength."[21] In Daniel 8:5 the prominent horn represents Alexander the Great. When it is broken four horns grow in its place representing the four generals who took power after Alexander's death. Finally, a new horn grows out of one of the four, and this little horn represents Antiochus IV Epiphanes. Given that horns signify the power of kings, the relevance of this sign for Antiochus is his power and authority, which he will use to abuse Israel. It is an uncomfortable image for the reader, as it forecasts the need for great faith during severe oppression.

Arguably, the most well-known signs in many apocalyptic visions are strange beasts. These beasts may not have been as strange to the original audience, but as they were not real animals, they would still have required imagination to be visualized. The four beasts of the vision of Daniel 7 may have ancient Near Eastern

---

2010), 82.

18 Andrew E. Hill, *Daniel*, Expositor's Bible Commentary, rev. ed. (Zondervan, 2008), 148.

19 Ibid.

20 Carson, *Scandalous*, 83.

21 Murphy, *Apocalypticism*, 80.

(ANE) parallels, and they certainly stand for kingdoms. For example, Hill notes that "The winged-lion (v. 4a) was a familiar motif in Babylonian art, and the lion and eagle as symbols of speed and strength are still widely recognized."[22] The fourth beast in that vision is only described in terms of the rhetorical impact: "...suddenly a fourth beast appeared, frightening and dreadful, and incredibly strong, with large iron teeth" (Dan 7:7). Here the text guides us to the right focus for the vision: this kingdom is scary strong.

With these strange beasts, the temptation will be for the congregation to be distracted by the foreign nature of the image and thus miss the point of relevance. Using media can be helpful for visualization, but be careful of distraction from the reason the sign is used. In the case of Daniel 7 Babylonian mythology is important background on one hand, but it is hardly necessary to feel the impact of the beasts in the vision. The best homiletic strategy here may be to only use the cultural data needed for the audience to appreciate the rhetorical force of the sign.

Natural Elements

Not only do individuals and animals take on roles in apocalyptic visions, but natural elements themselves do as well. Ryken notes: "In the strange and frequently surrealistic world of visionary literature, virtually any aspect of creation can become a participant in the ongoing drama of God's judgments and redemption."[23] This natural imagery is not meant to be understood as a literal depiction of future or past events. As Carson clarifies: "Rather, this is part of apocalyptic metaphor that derives from Hebrew poetry in which all of nature gets involved in everything. When things go well, the hills dance and the trees clap their hands. When things are bad, the stars fall from the sky, and nature falls into disarray."[24] Congregations may need help clarifying expectations regarding natural phenomena in apocalyptic visions. It is crucial to note that

---

22 Hill, *Daniel*, 134.
23 Leland Ryken, *How to Read the Bible as Literature* (Zondervan, 1984), 169.
24 Carson, *Scandalous*, 83.

the symbolic role of nature does not diminish the fact that the referent of the sign, judgment, or victory, is or will be a literal reality.

For example, when stars fall from the sky, the referent is chaos, disarray, and judgment. In Daniel 8:10 the little horn "grew as high as the heavenly army, made some of the army and some of the stars fall to the earth, and trampled them." In this vision some interpreters take the stars to be a reference to angels, a biblical image used elsewhere.[25] Others take it more generally as a reference to cataclysmic conflict.

The sea in ANE mythology is associated with chaos. This symbolism carries over seamlessly to apocalyptic visions. In both Daniel 7 and Revelation 13 beasts arise out of the sea. Commenting on Daniel 7, Hill highlights that this is no normal storm on the Mediterranean: "The emergence of 'four beasts' (v. 3), unnatural animal figures, from the churning waters brings an 'other-worldly' dimension to the vision."[26] The enemies of God's people arise from chaos to thwart his will. Mounce notes that this same imagery applies to Revelation 13: "Yet the ancient world commonly associated the sea with evil, and for the last great enemy of God's people to arise from the reservoir of chaos would be entirely appropriate."[27] It is no surprise that in the new earth the sea will be no more (Rev 21:1). Clarifying the symbolic nature of the sea in apocalyptic visions will help the audience appreciate the rebellion depicted in the vision. These beasts arising from the sea are challenging the authority of God and need to be understood in that light.

Props

Inanimate objects also feature in many apocalyptic visions. In most cases the relevance of such signs is clear from other biblical usage of the terms. Keep in mind that lower levels of biblical literacy will increase the need to offer brief insights into the background of such images for modern audiences. As with many signs, well

---

25 John C. Collins, *Daniel with an Introduction to Apocalyptic Literature* (Eerdmans, 1984), 333.

26 Hill, *Daniel,* 134.

27 Robert Mounce, *The Book of Revelation,* rev. ed. (Eerdmans, 1997), 244.

done visual aids used with discretion can quickly bring people up to speed on the visual of the sign. For some signs (e.g., crowns, thrones) the symbolism is obvious. For others the cultural significance will need some level of explanation. For example, the flying scroll in Zechariah 5:1–2 represents the law of God. That connection may not be obvious to many contemporary hearers.

Returning to the example of the lampstands that feature in Zechariah's fifth vision and the beginning of Revelation, note that the lampstand in view is the temple or tabernacle lampstand, the menorah. In John's apocalypse seven lampstands represent seven churches. Beale clarifies how the sign relates to the referent in both Zechariah and Revelation: "In Zech. 4:2–6 the lampstand with its seven lamps is a figurative synecdoche: part of the temple furniture stands for the whole temple, which by extension also represents faithful Israel (cf. Zech. 4:6–9)...."[28] In Zechariah's vision the lampstand is fueled by oil which is a symbol of the Spirit. In Revelation, Jesus is in the midst of the lampstands. This imagery delivers a robust concept in a small package: Jesus, through the Spirit, is at work in the church.

Books (or scrolls) in apocalyptic visions connote the sovereignty of God, often with an emphasis on judgment. Murphy clarifies the several ways books are used in apocalyptic texts: "They may contain the names of those who enjoy God's favor, they may record deeds, or they may lay out eschatological events."[29] God is sovereign over the events of history, over who receives eternal blessing, and over who is judged. In Ezekiel's first vision, God commands him to eat a scroll that is sweet. The scroll contains the message he must deliver to Israel in exile. The message itself is a message of judgment and mourning, but it is sweet as it prepares the people of God for repentance. This same prophetic sign act of eating a book occurs in Revelation 10:9–10. There John is warned the book will be bitter in his stomach, but sweet in his mouth. The sweetness pictures the goodness of God's Word—to those who believe it is sweeter than honey (Ps 19:11). The bitterness reflects the acknowledgement that the message is one of God's judgment. Wright observes,

---

28 G.K. Beale, *The Book of Revelation*, NIGTC (Eerdmans, 1999), 206.
29 Murphy, *Apocalypticism*, 80–81.

"'Eating the scroll' is a vivid metaphor for the way in which the prophet, then or indeed today, can only speak God's word insofar as it has become part of the prophet's own life."[30] In these visions the emphasis is simultaneously on the goodness of God's message even though it includes confrontation and judgment.

Angelic Actions

In addition to functioning as the vision mediators, angels also appear in various other roles in apocalyptic visions.[31] Angels stand apart from other characters in apocalyptic visions in that they are not symbolic in themselves, but their actions may be. In the vision they function like the prophet: they participate in the vision but do not represent someone or something else. Angels reveal a previously hidden reality to the vision recipients. Like Satan in Revelation 12, their actions in a vision may be symbolic for actions in real time and space.

In a sermon on an apocalyptic vision, focus on the purpose of the angelic action. Why are they doing what they are doing? One danger in preaching about angels in a philosophically modern context is skepticism in the audience regarding the supernatural. In these visions the importance of angels is not merely that they exist, but what they are doing in advancing the will of God.

Angels often serve as God's messengers, delivering his word to people. As such their actions are symbolic in that they represent past or future communication from God to people. In Revelation 14:6–12 three angels shout messages to the inhabitants of the earth. These messages share the gospel, announce the judgment of the wicked, and warn those who worship the beast. In the vision they fly over the earth crying out to humanity. From the perspective of the vision, this action symbolizes the real sharing of those messages, but it need not mean that angels will literally fly over the earth shouting to its inhabitants. It is the content of the message that is most important in this part of John's vision. He clarifies that the reason for this vision is to foster the endurance of the church:

---

30 Wright, *Revelation*, 94.
31 See Chapter 2 for more on angels as the mediators of apocalyptic visions.

"This calls for endurance from the saints, who keep God's commands and their faith in Jesus" (Rev 14:12).

Angels also serve by protecting the people of God. In Daniel 10:13 the angel mediating the vision reports to Daniel that he was preoccupied in spiritual warfare with other spiritual beings: "But the prince of the kingdom of Persia opposed me for twenty-one days. Then Michael, one of the chief princes, came to help me after I had been left there with the kings of Persia." While it may seem like a passing detail in the buildup to the vision proper, the reality of angels battling for the sake of God's people is relevant to the main point of this vision. In chapter 11, Daniel is shown a disturbing future in which Israel is essentially a pawn in the conflict between the Seleucid and Ptolemaic kingdoms. The vision makes clear they will suffer greatly during this time, yet they should persevere in faith because God has not forgotten them—angels are still waging war on their behalf.

Most often in apocalyptic visions angels serve as the agents of judgment, delivering God's wrath to the wicked. In Zechariah's first vision he sees different colored horses and riders going throughout the earth. They announce the world is at peace, but the Lord is angry with the enemies of Israel (Zech 1:8–17). In Revelation 6:1–8 we find a similar image of four horses with riders executing the judgment of God in various ways. Be mindful that images of God's messengers bringing judgment to the earth are often disturbing or unsettling for listeners. Even so, there are essential truths people need encapsulated in these images, such as God will punish the wicked and he has not forgotten the persecuted.[32] In sermons on visions with angels bringing about the judgment of God, point out the need for justice in every level of society and draw connections to ways hearers may have experienced or caused injustice.

Spiritually Significant Numbers

Numbers also function as signs in apocalyptic literature. This device is controversial, because the divide is deep between Christian

---

[32] See Chapter 5 for dealing with God's judgment of evil in apocalyptic visions.

interpreters who believe these numbers must be interpreted in a strictly literal fashion and those who believe these numbers should be interpreted figuratively. Are the lengths of time found in apocalyptic visions literal or symbolic? If by literal we mean "corresponding to a real chunk of time," then the answer is both. If by literal we mean "having a one-to-one correspondence to actual time," then we have to choose. The same holds true for other numbers (e.g., number of gates in the New Jerusalem, number of lampstands, etc.).

Non-biblical apocalyptic literature helps us here by showing us that the figurative use of numbers is a known strategy of apocalyptic literature in general. For example, Thomas McComiskey applies the ANE idea of completeness associated with the number seven to Daniel's 70 weeks. Regarding time frames given in sevens he concludes: "The action progresses until it culminates in the event of greatest importance in the seventh period."[33] He goes on to cite examples from 1 Enoch, the Dead Sea Scrolls, and the Testament of Levi where long periods of time are broken into non-literal chunks of ten or seven.[34] If the number is related to seven, the significance would have been perfection or completeness. If the number is related to ten, the significance would have been order, God's sovereign rule over history. This usage is found in "The Apocalypse of Weeks" in 1 Enoch 91:12–17, where notably history has ten periods. Stephen Reid describes how the seventh "week" is significant: "The description of the salvation of the seventh week is the bridge between the past and the future salvation described in the announcement of judgment in the second half of the apocalyptic timetable."[35] The use of numbers in non-biblical apocalyptic literature thus reveals a special use of numbers that bears theological symbolic significance: they communicate assumptions about the way God has ordered time and the universe.

Of course, the fact that certain numbers carried spiritual symbolic significance does not mean they cannot be taken literally.

---

33 Thomas McComiskey, "The Seventy 'Weeks' of Daniel Against the Background of Ancient Near Eastern Literature," *Westminster Theological Journal* 47 (1985): 39.

34 Ibid., 42.

35 Stephen B. Reid, "The Ten Week Apocalypse and the Book of Dream Visions," in *Journal for the Study of Judaism* 16.2 (1985): 195.

Nevertheless, even if the numbers are taken literally, they still would have had a rhetorical effect on the audience.[36] An example of this principle at work is the twelve gates and twelve foundations of the New Jerusalem in Revelation 21. John explains that the gates were named for the twelve tribes of Israel, and the foundations for the twelve apostles (Rev 21:12, 14). These numbers are meant to be understood literally (at least as far as the vision goes), and yet they also bear spiritual significance, standing for the tribes of Israel and apostles.

Homiletical Strategy 5: Paint the Picture

Equipped with the knowledge of how signs and symbols work in apocalyptic, the challenge remains to explain them effectively in a sermon. When preaching on apocalyptic visions, paint the picture that the vision presents. Strive to make the characters and props in the text clear. Visualization of apocalyptic imagery is one potential area where modern hearers are significantly handicapped. Not only are the dramatic beasts of Daniel 7 difficult to envision, but they also stand for something else—specific earthly kingdoms. The preacher needs to help the congregation in comprehending the imagery and interpreting its significance.

The biblical and ANE world of apocalyptic includes imagery known to its original hearers but not necessarily to modern hearers. Accurately and creatively filling in the cultural blanks for the audience enables them to frame the vision in their minds. This work engages the imagination of the audience. Gene Veith defines imagination as "the power of the mind to form a mental image, that is, to think in pictures or other sensory representations."[37] Building on that definition, Matthew Ristuccia argues that it is precisely the engagement of the imagination that makes apocalyptic visions (particularly those of Ezekiel) effective. He suggests that Israel in

---

36 I take the 70 weeks of Daniel to be literal "weeks" of years (that is, seven-year periods) without any gap, but this does not negate the spiritual significance of the numbers.

37 Gene Edward Veith Jr. and Matthew P. Ristuccia, *Imagination Redeemed* (Crossway, 2015), 13.

exile needed more than just an oracle; "Instead, they needed to see what they could not see: God's loyal providence."[38]

The purpose of engaging the imagination is to impact the hearts of hearers. Imagination is one avenue to engage affections. We need to remember that the act of preaching is not merely an intellectual exercise. Jonathan Edwards' philosophy of preaching was built on the idea that sermons are meant to impact affections, not only minds:

> God hath appointed a particular and lively application of his word, in the preaching of it, as a fit means to affect sinners with the importance of religion, their own misery, the necessity of a remedy, and the glory and sufficiency of a remedy provided; to stir up the pure minds of the saints, quicken their affections by often bringing the great things of religion to their remembrance, and setting them in their proper colours, though they know them, and have been fully instructed in them already.[39]

Thus, a key task in preaching apocalyptic is engaging the minds and hearts of hearers by painting the picture of apocalyptic imagery. Do so by personalizing a generic sign, using vivid language and imagery, using analogies, and being clear about the purpose of symbolic numbers.

Personalize a Generic Sign

Sometimes a sign that stands for a generic concept or group needs to be personalized. Consider again the example of the woman in the basket (Zech 5:5–11), who stands for wickedness. In this case preachers should be careful to not give the impression that wickedness is somehow related to femininity. This character serves to personify Israel's evil and its removal. The focus is on where evil

---

[38] Ibid., 29.
[39] Jonathan Edwards, "A Treatise Concerning Religious Affections in Three Parts," in *Works of Jonathan Edwards* (Banner of Truth Trust, 1995), 1:242, electronic ed.

belongs: not in the people of God but in Babylon. One way to personalize the image for the congregation is to use several examples relevant to the audience:

> This woman in a basket could be any of us. It could be the man defrauding a customer at work. It could be the woman gossiping at Bible study. It could be the young man in front of a computer late Friday night. It could be the preacher puffed up with pride. No matter who it is, sin doesn't belong in God's people.

Use Vivid Language and Imagery

Often apocalyptic images were used because they were so vivid to the original audience. Note the example of the nations of Greece and Medo-Persia in Daniel 8 presented as rams and goats to convey power and agility. Modern audiences may not think of power and agility when they think of rams and goats; the sermon should point them in that direction. Use vivid language to bring the image to life. These animals represent the military might of massive empires for a reason. For example:

> When we think of goats and rams, we might think of idyllic ranch scenes or cute farm animals or a petting zoo. But that's not how this ram and goat are presented. A closer image might be the ferocious scene of two rams waging war with their horns. These animals are supposed to bring to mind power, agility, speed, and the grit that it takes to dominate a foe.

Use Analogies

Analogies are the best way to make the meaning of signs clear when they convey concepts. For example, in Revelation 12:6 and 14 the wilderness is used as the safe haven for the church. This imagery is anchored in God's provision for Israel in the wilderness after the Exodus. Andrew Naselli explains that the wilderness in this example "symbolizes a place where God tests, protects, and miraculously nourishes his people."[40] Mounce agrees and describes how the focus of this imagery is on God's provision:

> The intent of the verse, however, is not so much the flight of the church as the provision of God for her sustenance. To the Jewish people the wilderness spoke of divine provision and intimate fellowship.... For John's readers the wilderness in this context would not suggest a desert waste inhabited by evil spirits and unclean beasts, but a place of spiritual refuge.[41]

Modern hearers will likely not associate wilderness with provision, so the preacher's task is to help them see this place through a biblical lens. Consider using an analogy of a place where someone was in great need and God provided—places associated with that event conjure hope, not despair:

> The wilderness here functions like Interstate 5 for me back in 2004. My truck broke down and I had to coast to the shoulder. Sitting there alone in the days before cell phones I was keenly aware of my need. Yet not far off was a call box provided for just such occasions. I called a dear friend who came to my rescue. Now every time I drive by or think of that spot on the road I don't think of need; I think of provision. This is the promise of God to the church. Yes, Satan is raging against us, but God will provide.

Be Clear with Numbers

Painting the picture with numbers in apocalyptic visions does not mean presenting infamous chronological charts for an eschatological scheme. On the contrary, draw out the symbolic importance of certain numbers. This will help the audience appreciate what these numbers are doing in the vision.

One number that occurs both in Daniel and Revelation is 1,260

---

40 Andrew David Naselli, *The Serpent and the Serpent Slayer* (Crossway, 2020), 116.

41 Mounce, *Revelation*, 234.

days (or three and a half years).⁴² D.A. Carson notes how cultures have periods of time that carry "symbol-laden value."⁴³ In Daniel this period of time was the time of suffering of Israel under Antiochus IV Epiphanes. Naselli summarizes that 1,260 days here symbolizes "a period of intense suffering for God's people before God delivers them."⁴⁴ To acknowledge this symbolic use of numbers is not to jettison the literal referent of the vision. Rather, it helps the reader appreciate the nature of what has happened, is happening, or will happen in history.

Whether a given number in a biblical apocalyptic text is literal or not is a matter for exegetical investigation. Whatever decision the exegete comes to, we should not ignore the spiritual significance of these numbers. As a strategy, these numbers address the specifics of the audience's situation. They communicated hope to an audience in a situation of hopelessness, suffering, or persecution. In such times people would understandably ask "How long, O Lord, do we have to endure this?" Often, biblical apocalyptic texts answer that question. Recall that Daniel's 70 weeks of years is an answer to his prayer regarding the 70 years of exile prophesied by Jeremiah. The "exile" was not just a matter of displacement, but it was a matter of spiritual sickness for which the only cure was the arrival of the Messiah at God's appointed time.

Summary of Homiletical Strategy 5

God has given the church not only the genre of apocalyptic but also the specific details of each vision, including signs, symbols, and numbers. Sermons that paint the picture of apocalyptic visions marked by clarity with honesty and humility will provide a needed wake up call to the church while avoiding the pitfall of eschatological rabbit holes. Paint the picture by:

- personalizing a generic sign,
- using vivid language and imagery,

---

42 The "time and times and half a time" familiar from the KJV.
43 Carson, *Scandalous*, 86.
44 Naselli, *The Serpent and the Serpent Slayer*, 114.

- using analogies,
- being clear about the purpose of symbolic numbers.

Homiletical Strategy 6: Follow the Vision Interpreter

In dealing with signs, symbols, and numbers in apocalyptic we also need to follow the heavenly interpreter. Following the interpreter means allowing the God-given text and vision interpretation to drive our explanation of signs and symbols. Far too often preachers run wild hermeneutically and homiletically with the symbols in apocalyptic. Richard Taylor cautions against baseless interpretations of the symbolic elements in apocalyptic: "The language of symbolism can lose its effectiveness and become a playground for interpretational gymnastics that wind up distorting rather than illumining the text."[45]

The heavenly mediator of apocalyptic visions is a built-in defense against such "interpretational gymnastics." The fact that in many apocalyptic visions the key symbolic elements are interpreted (often by the heavenly mediator) is of immense help to the preacher. We can follow the interpreter by:

- explaining the nature of signs and symbols,
- being clear about referents that are explicitly identified in the text,
- focusing on why a sign is used for a referent,
- avoiding overselling hypothetical identification of sign referents,
- dealing directly with signs that may be unusual or controversial to the audience,
- refusing to generalize the message of the vision.

Explain the Nature of Signs and Symbols

When we preach on apocalyptic visions, we have spent hours of study on the interpretation and application of the text, not to mention the years of study in preparation for ministry, but we must remember that the overwhelming majority of our audience has not

---

[45] Richard A. Taylor, *Interpreting Apocalyptic Literature* (Kregel, 2016), 127.

studied or been taught how to read and understand apocalyptic visions. In sermons on apocalyptic it is worth a few minutes to bring the audience up to speed on the basics of interpreting signs.

D.A. Carson does this well in a sermon on Revelation 12. Notice how in just a few sentences he explains how signs work and gives a few examples that will be relevant to the text at hand:

> Well in apocalyptic there are a lot of standard symbols that you get to know. For example, every time you find a horn it means either a king or a kingdom. Numbers are deeply symbolic; you have seven horns it means a perfection of kingly authority or the like. Twelve in this book regularly has to do with the twelve tribes of Israel or the twelve apostles of the New Covenant.... The natural elements: the stars swept out of the heaven does not mean that the author really thinks that stars are tiny things that can be swept out of the heavens. It's a way of saying a disaster is taking place. And conversely, when everything is going well, then the trees are dancing for joy and the hills are clapping their hands. So you have to get to know how the language works to make sense of it.[46]

In the process of equipping the audience to think about these signs and symbols be careful not to take too long. A short primer can quickly devolve into a ten-minute lecture on hermeneutics. Taking a few extra minutes in sermon preparation to craft an intro to signs and symbols will save time in the pulpit and headache in the pew. In preparation ask: "How can I concisely explain this to those who have never heard of an apocalyptic vision? What terms or signs will be foreign to my audience?"

Be Clear on What Is Clear

Another way to follow the interpreter in sermons on apocalyptic is to be clear about referents that are made clear in the vision. When

---

46 D.A. Carson, "The Strange Triumph of a Slaughtered Lamb," https://resources.thegospelcoalition.org/library/the-strange-triumph-of-a-slaughtered-lamb-revelation-12-part-2-of-5.

the text offers clarity, the sermon should reflect that clarity. One pitfall in sermons on apocalyptic is neglecting what is clear and focusing on what is unclear. Emphasizing clearly identified referents allows the sermon to stand on solid ground and prevents misapplication of the text. For example, the identity of the seven spirits of God in Revelation 3:1 and 4:5 is not clear. If the main point of your sermon rests on your view of these spirits, and you are wrong, then your sermon points the congregation in the wrong direction.

Perhaps some signs and symbols frustrate us because we unnecessarily impose upon ourselves the exegetical and homiletic burden of identifying the referent of every aspect of the vision. Like some details in parables, sometimes a sign is just a prop in the aesthetic of the vision. Leland Ryken reminds us to focus on the sum total of the vision: "Nor should we allegorize every detail in a passage unless there is a hint that we are intended to do so. Often it is the total impact of a scene or action that conveys the meaning."[47] Tunnel vision on one aspect of a vision easily leads to distortion of the focus of vision in the sermon as a whole. This danger makes it all the more important to be clear on the overall narrative of the vision when identifying signs and their referents.

A sermon on apocalyptic should include further explanation when it comes to being clear on important biblical characters or imagery. For example, in Revelation 12 the apostle John is given a vision that includes a dragon that is identified as Satan: "So the great dragon was thrown out—the ancient serpent, who is called the devil and Satan, the one who deceives the whole world" (Rev 12:9). For many, the rich biblical background of the image of Satan as a dragon is obvious, but for others it is not. A brief summary of Satan's role in the Bible will be helpful for the audience. After such an explanation be sure to highlight the role of Satan in this particular vision—emphasizing what John emphasizes in his record. In this case Satan is unsuccessful in his attempt to thwart the mission of the Messiah.

In some visions, signs are not identified until much later in the text. For example, in Daniel 8 the vision itself runs from 8:1–14 and the interpretation by the guide from 8:15–27. Being clear in

---

47 Ryken, *How to Read*, 174.

examples like this may mean providing the interpretation ahead of time by giving spoilers for the audience about the identification of signs in the vision. Plan ahead of time how to budget chunks of text and where to include identification of signs and symbols. Will you read the entire vision and the interpretation? Will you break it up into sections? Leaving signs and symbols unidentified for too long in a sermon can effectually leave the audience in the dark. Doing so may be helpful to sustain tension, but beware unintentionally leaving the audience uninformed.

For Daniel 8, one homiletic option is to clearly explain that the two-horned ram stands for the kings of Media and Persia and the horn of the shaggy goat stands for Alexander the Great right from the outset. This will minimize confusion as you move through the vision details. Then you can move on to address the significance of the signs and begin to apply the vision to the lives of the audience.

Focus on the Why

What is often significant in a vision is why a particular sign stands for its referent. Rather than merely focusing on the explanation of the sign, the sermon will need to make clear the connection between the sign and the referent as it relates to the vision as a whole. The two "sons of oil" in Zechariah's fifth vision illustrate this point. In Zechariah 4 the prophet sees a vision of a lampstand, two olive trees, and a bowl. Zechariah asks his angelic vision guide for clarification on the identity of the olive trees: "I asked him, 'What are the two olive trees on the right and left of the lampstand?' And I questioned him further, 'What are the two streams of the olive trees, from which the golden oil is pouring through the two golden conduits?'" (Zech 4:11–12). The angel answered: "These are the two anointed ones who stand by the Lord of the whole earth" (Zech 4:14). It is clear from the context that the referents are the high priest Joshua and the leader Zerubbabel (of Davidic lineage), but what is the link?

The symbolism surrounding the olive oil connects the two roles of (royal) leader and high priest to the olive trees. The word for oil in Zechariah 4:14 is יִצְהָר (*yatzhar*), which may be an "archaic equivalent" to the more common term שֶׁמֶן (shemen).⁴⁸ David Petersen observes that יִצְהָר (yitzhar) is not used of anointing oil in the OT but rather of agricultural blessing. He notes "...this particular noun is regularly used in a stereotypical list ('grain, wine, oil') to indicate the natural and bountiful harvest of Syria-Palestine."⁴⁹ This usage may clarify the reason for the image. Carol and Eric Meyers draw a similar conclusion about יִצְהָר (yitzhar): it "has a specific connotation; it designates the fresh new oil of olives.... 'New oil' is associated with the blessing that comes with God's favor as crops produce their full yield."⁵⁰ Thus the focus is that Joshua and Zerubbabel are empowered by the Spirit of God to be agents of blessing as they finish the reconstruction of the temple (Zech 4:6).⁵¹

This exegetical homework might yield a paragraph in a sermon like this:

> The word for oil used here has connotations of God's blessing through provision of a harvest. These 'sons of oil' will be the means by which God blesses Israel's return to the land from exile. How? By facilitating the temple's reconstruction. The Spirit of God will empower them to finish the work.

Avoid Overselling Uncertain Identifications of Signs and Symbols

What about when a sign's referent is not made clear? If the identity of a sign's referent is not clearly stated in the vision, we should be hesitant and humble about overselling a theory on the identity of a given sign. D. Brent Sandy and Martin Abegg Jr. caution against haphazard interpretations of apocalyptic visions: "The apocalyptic

---

48 HALOT, 427.

49 David L. Petersen, *Haggai and Zechariah 1–8* (Westminster, 1984), 230.

50 Carol L. Meyers and Eric M. Meyers, *Haggai, Zechariah 1–8* (Yale University Press, 1987), 258.

51 An alternative view of the significance of the olive oil imagery is based on fact that priests and kings would have been anointed by oil. In such cases, however, the term שֶׁמֶן (shemen) would be expected. For a defense of this view see Joyce G. Baldwin, *Haggai, Zechariah and Malachi*, TOTC (IVP Academic, 1972), 132.

genre has been subjected to some of the most fallacious interpretations imaginable, largely because Christians are often not careful to understand it as intended and as originally heard."[52] In other words, paying close attention to the details and background of the passage helps us avoid sketchy interpretations of signs.

Be hesitant to build a sermon on a new or contested interpretation of a sign. If the main idea of a sermon depends on a novel or highly debated identification of a sign's reference, then the danger is high that the sermon is straying from the intent of the biblical author. Humility and honesty serve the preacher and the congregation well in these cases. Often, spending time in a sermon on the complexities of a vision is a waste of time. Allow the focus of the text itself to drive decision making on how much explanation is needed on minor elements in the vision.

Interpreting signs that are not identified in the text may require some further exegetical work. Bandy provides a helpful step-by-step process for interpreting signs focusing on Revelation. Should the text or the guide in the vision not identify a referent, he recommends determining if the sign is an allusion to the OT, comparing it with non-canonical apocalyptic texts, and looking for connections between the sign and the cultural or historical context of the work.[53] Consulting commentaries and other reference works may provide compelling arguments for drawing reasonable conclusions.

In visions where it is necessary to reference different options for a debated sign referent, watch out for an arrogant tone. Be willing to say: "There are two main options for what this sign stands for. I think the best option is...." When dealing with multiple options for a sign referent be sure to remind the congregation of the main idea of the vision. The main idea of a vision is usually not affected by a debatable sign referent. Consider adding a focusing statement: "While we may not be certain about what this sign represents, we know the focus of the vision is...."

---

52 D. Brent Sandy and Martin G. Abegg Jr., "Apocalyptic," in *Cracking Old Testament Codes,* ed. D. Brent Sandy and Ronald L. Giese Jr. (Broadman & Holman, 1995), 187.

53 Bandy, "The Hermeneutics of Symbolism," 51–53.

Avoid being over-confident when dealing with signs whose referents are highly debated. Consider the example in Revelation 1:12, where the apostle John sees seven golden lampstands in his vision. In Revelation 1:20 he is told "…the seven lampstands are the seven churches." Why do lampstands represent churches? Robert Mounce suggests, "The purpose of the church is to bear the light of the divine presence in a darkened world."[54] Are there further links in the OT that might lend clarity? Beale links this sign to Zechariah 4:2 and 10. He suggests the import of the sign is the focus on God's Spirit being present in the church and "the endtime temple has been inaugurated in the church" (cf. Rev 1:4; 4:5).[55] The strength of Beale's interpretation is that it accounts for why a significant piece of temple furniture would now be used to represent churches.[56]

In this example both Mounce's and Beale's views have merit. The two are not mutually exclusive: the church bears the light of God's presence by virtue of the Spirit. The preacher will need to weigh the options and draw a conclusion, then consider how much background information is needed for the audience to understand and apply the text. In the sermon itself do not feel obligated to give the congregation all of the interpretive options. A better option is to summarize the one or two main reasons the sign is used and focus on the impact to the message of the vision.

Deal with Controversial, Unfamiliar, or Unusual Signs

Inevitably, in some visions certain aspects will be controversial, unfamiliar, or unusual to an audience. Addressing these signs directly is ideal. This strategy will answer questions the audience may already be asking, and it will clear up confusion to allow for greater understanding of the message of the vision. Dealing with these foreign images may be accomplished by using visual aids,

---

54 Mounce, *Revelation*, 57.
55 Beale, *Revelation*, 207.
56 A further interpretive question in this text is whether the seven churches addressed here stand as representative of all churches. This question is one step past dealing with the sign itself, and thus beyond the scope of this chapter.

giving clear explanation, acknowledging uncertain referents, and honestly disclosing interpretive differences.

Unfamiliar signs will need description or modern analogies to help the congregation feel their impact. In both Zechariah's fifth vision and in Revelation 1 a lampstand is a key sign. In this case a visual aid would quickly allow the congregation to visualize the lampstand. Consider using helpful images in a slide or handout to engage the audience's imagination. While media use can be a great help, be careful of too much emphasis on the media and not enough on the vision in the text itself. The main reason to use visual aids is to equip the congregation to picture the vision in their minds without confusion or misunderstanding. Many visual aids may be interesting but not necessarily helpful for the purpose of the sermon.

Acknowledging controversial signs in eschatology is another way to help the congregation stay focused on the message of the vision. One such sign is the 1000-year reign of Christ described in Revelation 20:1–6. Many congregants will already be aware that views on this millennial kingdom constitute a major divide in Christian interpretation while others will not. Being upfront about aspects on which Christian interpreters agree and disagree will help the congregation think clearly throughout the sermon. Neglecting to be clear at the outset could result in the audience wondering about the preacher's position rather than listening to the text. In cases like this, also consider acknowledging which aspects of the vision's application are highly impacted by different interpretive schemes. Honest, humble clarity in matters of eschatology will serve the congregation well as they seek to believe and apply these unusual parts of God's Word.

Refuse to Generalize the Message

Although I have cautioned against making too much of incidental details, you do not want to err in the opposite direction: making too little of the details and settling for a vague generalized message. Flattening a vision by glossing over or simply neglecting to deal with signs in the vision may distort the message of the text. One over-generalized message often used when preaching apocalyptic texts is the reality that God ultimately wins in the end. While this is no doubt true, apocalyptic visions focus on specific aspects of that victory. How will God win? Why? What is the effect on believers? These are the areas of interest in apocalyptic visions, and to let the text drive the sermon we must be willing to do the hard work of studying and listening to the details of the text.

In a sermon on Revelation 12:1–6, Peter Vaught identifies the referent of the sign of the dragon in 12:3 as the general concept of evil. He states: "Friends, the red dragon is a frightening face of evil."[57] He goes on to say: "The evil it represents has shown itself to be war, torture, persecution, political upheaval, abuse, and destruction."[58] The problem with this generalization is that in Revelation 12:9 the red dragon is explicitly identified as "the ancient serpent, who is called the devil and Satan, the one who deceives the whole world." Vaught has confused the cause for the effect in his sermon, and the result is a distortion of the message of the vision. John is not relating to us a vision of generic evil seeking to destroy the Messiah. He is relating to us a vision of Satan actively scheming to destroy Jesus and his bride. Our enemy is not the concept of evil, it is the ancient serpent and his deceiving the world. Vaught's sermon leaves the audience with a distorted view of the cause of evil and misses the main thrust of the message.

Summary of Homiletical Strategy 6

We have learned that following the angelic interpreter is an essential aspect of presenting the signs and symbols in apocalyptic visions. Following the angelic interpreter means listening carefully to the text of the vision. Do this by:

- explaining the nature of signs and symbols,
- being clear about referents that are explicitly identified in the text,

---

[57] Peter Vaught, "Within Reach of the Dragon," in *Preaching Through the Apocalypse*, ed. Cornish R. Rogers and Joseph R. Jeter Jr. (Chalice, 1992), 123.
[58] Ibid.

- focusing on why a sign is used for a referent,
- avoiding dubious hypothetical identification of sign referents,
- dealing directly with signs that may be unusual or controversial to the audience,
- refusing to generalize the message of the vision.

Experienced guides make all the difference in navigating the figurative language of apocalyptic visions. The pictorial power of signs and the essential aid of heaven-sent vision mediators point us to sure footing in interpretation and application in sermons on apocalyptic. The next critical aspect in catching and casting the vision is embracing the revolutionary worldview of apocalyptic visions.

For Further Study

Bandy, Alan. "The Hermeneutics of Symbolism: How to Interpret the Symbols of John's Apocalypse." *Southern Baptist Journal of Theology* 14.1 (2010): 46–58.

Bauckham, Richard. *The Climax of Prophecy.* T&T Clark, 1993.

Sandy, Brent D. *Plowshares & Pruning Hooks: Rethinking the Language of Biblical Prophecy and Apocalyptic.* InterVarsity, 2002, 103–128.

Talk about It

What is your position on eschatology? What are ways that position (or non-position!) influences how you approach the symbolic elements of apocalyptic visions?

Dig Deeper

Review Bandy's steps for identifying signs on pages 49–54 of his article "The Hermeneutics of Symbolism." Consider ways to incorporate these steps in your exegetical work on apocalyptic visions in sermon preparation.

Practice

Read the vision in Zechariah 5:1–11. Identify the signs and referents used in that vision. Consider ways a modern audience might struggle to understand each sign/referent pair. List one or two ways you can effectively use or explain each in a sermon.

5

Apocalyptic Transcendent Perspective: Good, Evil, and Revolutionary Thinking

> *From first to last, and not merely in the epilogue, Christianity is eschatology, is hope, forward looking and forward moving, and therefore also revolutionizing and transforming the present. The eschatological is not one element of Christianity, but it is the medium of Christian faith as such, the key in which everything in it is set, the glow that suffuses everything here in the dawn of an expected new day.*[1]
>
> Jürgen Moltmann

CATCHING THE VISION OF apocalyptic literature involves embracing a transcendent view of the world and our place in it. Casting that vision means preaching a sermon informed by the heavenly perspective on the world as it is and as it will be, as depicted in the biblical text. Just like our view of the ground changes when we take off in an airplane, so should our view of life change in light of biblical apocalyptic visions. Understanding and conveying the transcendent perspective of the vision enables us to see our circumstances differently.

Interpretive Insights

Apocalyptic visions are designed to facilitate a revolution in worldview. They help the audience reinterpret their circumstances in

---
1 Jürgen Moltmann, *Theology of Hope* (Fortress, 1993), 16.

light of the transcendent reality revealed to the prophet. These visions challenge the recipients to think beyond what they can see. The prophet is welcomed behind the curtain to see a heavenly perspective of his people's earthly circumstances. Apocalyptic literature is "intended to interpret present, earthly circumstances in light of the supernatural world and of the future, and to influence both the understanding and the behavior of the audience by means of divine authority."[2] The baseline assumption of the vision is that unseen heavenly realities should change the readers' interpretation and response to their current circumstances, enabling them to live by faith in their current circumstances.

The method is simple: revealing a heavenly perspective shines a divine light on earthly situations. Apocalyptic visions draw a clear line between good and evil. D. Brent Sandy and Martin Abegg Jr. note that apocalyptic is marked by "a dualistic perspective that categorizes things into contrasting elements such as good and evil, this age and the age to come."[3] This heavenly perspective exposes evil and reveals that the final word is coming. Frederick Murphy explains that this heavenly knowledge enables the vision recipients to see the dualistic nature of the universe: "Apocalyptic revelation has a spatial and a temporal aspect. The spatial aspect means that the seer receives special knowledge about the unseen world—the world of angels and demons, of God and Satan."[4] Apocalyptic literature offers a transcendent worldview in three ways: it provides a clean resolution to the problem of evil, it gives visions of the victory of God's people, and it gives visions of the judgment of the wicked.

A Resolution to the Problem of Evil

The apocalyptic worldview offers a clean resolution to the problem

---

[2] Adela Yarbro Collins, "Early Christian Apocalypticism: Introduction," *Seimeia* 36 (1986): 7.

[3] D. Brent Sandy and Martin G. Abegg Jr., "Apocalyptic," in *Cracking Old Testament Codes*, ed. D. Brent Sandy and Ronald L. Giese Jr. (Broadman & Holman, 1995), 180.

[4] Frederick J. Murphy, *Apocalypticism in the Bible and Its World: A Comprehensive Introduction* (Baker Academic, 2012), 203.

of evil. In stark contrast to moral confusion, canonical apocalyptic texts are unambiguous regarding the existence of evil and God's commitment to deal with it. Apocalyptic literature claims to reveal *the* line between good and evil. Whether it is the four chariots of Zechariah patrolling the earth imposing God's justice, or the seven bowls of God's wrath poured out in Revelation, these visions reveal that God will deal with evil. The black and white nature of the depiction of evil in canonical apocalyptic texts contrasts with the often-grey moral ambiguity of modern life.

This resolution speaks directly to people suffering. In such times many wonder: "Will these wrongs ever be set right?" Apocalyptic visions not only answer yes, they give a glorious picture of how. Evil is not just exposed in apocalyptic visions; it is dealt with decisively in order to facilitate a revolutionary worldview for the vision recipients. Thus, the prophet Ezekiel sees the Lord's angels destroying Jerusalem in judgment for idolatry (Ezek 8–11). Living in exile, the prophet Daniel sees the Son of Man descend to earth to render judgment and reign over competing earthly kingdoms (Dan 7:9–13). In post-exile Jerusalem Zechariah sees horsemen avenge Israel by attacking Babylon (Zech 6:1–8). This revolution in worldview is not merely an OT apocalyptic concern. In the NT, God gives the apostle John a vision of the judgment of Babylon, the representative of all sinful human culture (Rev 18:1–24).

Visions of Victory

In addition to a resolution to the problem of evil, apocalyptic visions often give glimpses of the transcendent reality of heaven. From the perspective of Isaiah, Daniel, Ezekiel, Zechariah, and John, the transcendent is real because they experienced it. Their experience was meant to be shared. The meaning and hope that come from the narrative of future victory they received is designed to provide meaning and hope for others. People sitting in exile in Babylon or in a cell in Asia Minor needed to know that God's grand story is more comedy than tragedy. These visions of victory provide a certain hope by revealing the kingdom of God and by showing the vindication of believers who have been persecuted.

As Thomas Long notes: "apocalyptic literature draws back the curtains and allows the reader to see the eschatological victory of God, which has already been achieved over whatever forces are, even at the moment, crippling the community of faith."[5]

This hope looks forward *temporally* and *teleologically*. Temporally, it is a future hope that is yet to be fully realized but will be. Our resurrection and the culmination of our salvation have not yet occurred. We look forward to that time because of God's purpose. Teleologically, God's glory will be manifested in the completion of the mission: the judgment of sin, redemption of the Church, and renewal of creation. As such, Christian hope is not a vague expression of positive thinking but involves looking forward to the concrete fulfillment of our salvation and restoration of creation.

Apocalyptic visions show the victory of the people of God in the establishment of God's kingdom. In Daniel 7:18 believers have a vested interest in the kingdom: "But the holy ones of the Most High will receive the kingdom and possess it forever, yes, forever and ever." The earth itself will be renewed, as seen in the renewal of the Judean wilderness and the Dead Sea by a new river flowing from the temple in Ezekiel 47:8–12 and the vision of the new heaven and earth in Revelation 21:1. The kingdom of God will have no sin, pain, or mourning as described in Revelation 21:4. The saints will dwell together with God without any barrier as depicted in Revelation 21:3 and Zechariah 2:6. These pictures of the glorious resolution of history are designed to give hope to believers in their present circumstances.[6]

Apocalyptic visions also preview the vindication of the church in the reversal of fortune of persecuted saints. In Daniel 7:27 the vision of God's judgment and displacement of earthly kingdoms culminates with the vindication of the saints, "The kingdom, dominion, and greatness of the kingdoms under all of heaven will be

---

5 Thomas Long, "Preaching Apocalyptic Literature," *Review and Expositor* 90 (1993): 376–377.

6 Different interpretations of the signs in these visions does not change their hope-giving function. If the renewal of the land in Ezekiel 40–48 is taken to be only a reference to Israel in the millennial kingdom the vision still gave hope to its original audience. See Chapter 7 for more on interpretive differences in application.

given to the people, the holy ones of the Most High." These holy ones are most likely the same ones who suffered persecution in Daniel 7:25. The message is clear: although believers may suffer now, ultimate victory is theirs by God's provision.

This reversal is also seen in the army of the Lamb in Revelation 14:1–4. Though slain in life, they paradoxically stand victorious with the Lamb. The world cannot rob believers of significance because significance is found in their connection to the Lamb. Believers may face economic and social persecution; they can be overlooked for promotions or shunned in society. Thus, what Larry Jones and Paul Sumney state regarding the original audience of apocalyptic texts is also true of postmodern believers: "They need a word of hope about the victory of God and about their participation in that victory."[7] God will not forget them no matter what kind of marginalization they suffer. Should they suffer the end of a martyr, they will not be forgotten by the Lord.

Visions of the Judgment of the Wicked

Apocalyptic visions also offer hope by pointing to God as the just judge. In one sense these visions effectively give a preview of the judgment of the wicked—a major theme in apocalyptic literature. God's judgment is depicted in the destruction of pagan culture with special focus on the violent and those who persecuted the church. Apocalyptic visions of justice culminate in the final judgment of all unbelievers, which functions as a warning to unbelievers and as a comfort to the church.

One key facet of God's judgment of the wicked is that it is sure even if the wicked seem indestructible at present. The destruction of pagan culture is a theme in the visions of Daniel and Revelation that reminds readers that God has not abdicated his throne and he will put powerful, wicked governments in their place. As seen above, in Daniel 7 the four beasts/kingdoms will ultimately be judged by God and replaced by his kingdom. In Revelation 17 and 18, John describes the destruction of Babylon, who is depicted

---

[7] Larry Paul Jones and Jerry L. Sumney, *Preaching Apocalyptic Texts* (Chalice, 1999), 106.

as the great harlot who led the entire earth in idolatry and immorality. These visions broadly address the reality that sin has resulted in corrupt governments. The narrative of Revelation 17–18 affirms that the system is broken, but it also adds the specific reason why: sin. The idolatry of the system needs to be dealt with, and in the vision, God will deal with it by destroying Babylon. God will not only deal with individual sinners, but also the entire sin-tainted system.

Homiletical Strategy 7: Offer Hope

The homiletic challenge with the transcendent perspective of apocalyptic is relevance. Any discussion of good and evil in a sermon demands an honest appraisal of the reality of suffering in the lives of the hearers. Some may be experiencing severe suffering, while others may have yet to experience it. Either way, the sermon must follow through to the intent of the vision by offering hope. The exposure of good and evil terminates in the righteous judgment of God. It is not enough to acknowledge that evil exists and people suffer, the sermon should point to God as the just judge of the universe as the basis of faith in the midst of suffering.

Offering genuine hope in spite of suffering is one way to craft a sermon on apocalyptic in light of its moral dualism and revolutionary purpose. The presence of God's judgment of evil in many apocalyptic visions can make many feel uncomfortable, but in a world broken by sin we need reminders that evil will not win the day. Offer hope by acknowledging the reality of evil and suffering in the world of the hearers, giving a preview of the coming victory of the people of God, and giving a preview of God's judgment of the wicked. Along the way, sermons on these visions should also identify faulty views of justice and ultimate victory.

Honestly Appraise Evil and Suffering

Exposing evil is a major function of apocalyptic visions, and any sermon on an apocalyptic vision needs to do the same. Speaking about evil and suffering presents two major homiletic challenges.

First, the default worldview of Western culture rejects moral standards. Sermons on apocalyptic may need to re-assert the existence of God's standard of right and wrong. Second, the difference in the scale of evil and suffering between the biblical and modern contexts might cause listeners to miss out on application to their lives. Therefore, sermons on apocalyptic will need to draw clear connections in application to contemporary circumstances.

Preaching about evil in a pluralistic culture means sermons may need to reestablish God's moral standard. D.A. Carson points out the dilemma:

> In the moral realm, there is very little consensus left in Western countries over the proper basis of moral behavior.... Personal and social ethics have been removed from the realms of truth and of structure of thought; they have not only been relativized, but they have been democratized and trivialized.[8]

People still assert that there is a right and wrong, but adjudicating between the two is increasingly difficult and often perceived to be unnecessary. This is especially true for evaluations of behavior based on religion. For example, speaking of evaluating religious truth claims, Hans Küng asserts: "Instead of an indifferentism for which everything is equally valid, let there be somewhat more *indifference* toward the alleged orthodoxy that makes itself the measure of the salvation or damnation of human beings...."[9] This hesitance to adopt any standard of judgment is incompatible with the worldview of apocalyptic.

Consider ways to remind hearers that right and wrong do exist. Perhaps use a contemporary or personal example to call attention to the fact that God is the one who determines right and wrong, or use general observations on injustice that allow listeners to fill the gaps. For example, in a sermon on the book of Revelation, Mark

---

8 D.A. Carson, *The Gagging of God: Christianity Confronts Pluralism* (Zondervan, 1996), 23.

9 Hans Küng, "What is True Religion? Toward an Ecumenical Criteriology," in *Toward a Universal Theology of Religion,* ed. Leonard Swidler (Orbis, 1987), 237, emphasis his.

Dever points out the reality of injustice in a contemporary legal setting:

> So, when we think of this idea of judgment, people today often have trouble with this, and I think I can understand why. Our justice is often insufficient. Our justice is uncertain. Our justice is often stopgap. Frankly it's sometimes wrong. We don't always catch even those that we know are guilty and when we do they get out and they often repeat their crime. The judgments that are often handed down seem insufficient. Sometimes they are simply wrong. In this world there is no perfect justice.[10]

Having affirmed the fact that evil and suffering exist, the task remains to connect the experience of the audience with the apocalyptic vision. On one hand it is likely that the suffering, marginalization, and persecution of the original vision recipients is worse than that of believers in Western culture. On the other hand, suffering is suffering. People today are just as much victims of evil as ever. In fact, apocalyptic visions may speak uniquely to certain contemporary circumstances.

Comparing or contrasting the context of the first readers to modern listeners will help clarify what aspects of evil and suffering need to be addressed in the sermon. C. Marvin Pate calls this identifying the "shared need" of the passage. He explains a two-step process to identify a shared need in an apocalyptic passage: "isolate the need(s) addressed in the historical and literary context of the passage; determine the need(s) contemporary listeners share with the original audience."[11] Put another way, consider what situation the author was addressing, and then ask how might your audience have a similar situation.

Sometimes these two sets of circumstances are not as far apart as they might first seem. For example, Daniel's visions are

---

10 Mark Dever, "What Are We Waiting For? The Message of Revelation," https://www.capitolhillbaptist.org/sermon/what-are-we-waiting-for-the-message-of-revelation.

11 C. Marvin Pate, *Interpreting Revelation and Other Apocalyptic Literature* (Kregel, 2016), 174.

addressed to Israelites in exile. They had lost everything and were forced to live as minorities in a foreign culture. Although most believers have not experienced the loss of their country or temple, they are marginalized in that they live in a context where belief in God is increasingly rare. Modern society is a secular society in that it is a society "where belief in God... is understood to be one option among others, and frequently not the easiest to embrace."[12] Charles Taylor is right, our age is a secular age. Christians breathe secular air, and increasingly find themselves in the minority and facing temptation to join the majority.

Acknowledging where suffering or marginalization exists opens a door of direct application of apocalyptic visions to the listeners' lives. Perhaps Christians in the audience increasingly feel like minorities in their culture. Perhaps they have lost jobs or homes and feel hopeless. When life circumstances are not what people expect or hope, loss of faith is often a byproduct. Can God be trusted? Apocalyptic visions offer answers that do not gloss over the hurt or pain people are experiencing.

The difference in experiencing persecution is one of scale, not of kind. For example, Adela Collins explains how John's vision in the book of Revelation reflects the circumstances of its first audience: "The persecution reflected in Revelation... seems to be nothing more than an example of the usual sporadic repression suffered by the Christians in the first two centuries."[13] The point of connection to a modern listener might be that they lost a job because they fell out of favor with an unbelieving boss, or they are being alienated by unbelieving family members because of their faith. Be careful when acknowledging suffering not to belittle the congregation's experience. While it may not be as severe as living under Nero, all persecution hurts.

Consider this example dealing with the trampling of the holy city and the martyrdom of the two witnesses in a sermon on Revelation 11:1–14:

---

12 Charles Taylor, *A Secular Age* (Harvard University Press, 2007), 3.
13 Adela Yarbro Collins, *Crisis and Catharsis: The Power of the Apocalypse* (Westminster, 1984), 73.

Like a toddler struggling to understand discipline from parents, often we struggle to understand why God would purpose for his church to suffer. This vision reveals there is much more going on. The same is true when the church suffers today, regardless of the intensity of persecution. Whether it's a local politician flexing muscle to be a pain or an unbelieving co-worker stirring up trouble, we can be confident that God has a plan, and he is trustworthy.

Carefully considering and comparing the situation of the vision's original readers with that of the audience helps show where the text most directly applies to them and creates an empathetic environment. As evil is exposed, the message of apocalyptic is God will deal with it in the end. To identify ways that truth intersects with the suffering and marginalization of the listener is to help them find hope.

Give Glimpses of Victory

A second way to offer hope in sermons on apocalyptic is to give glimpses of the victory of God's people. The visionary representation of God's ultimate victory is meant to inspire confidence in God despite present challenges for hearers. The fact that this victory is not fully realized is key to the hope-giving function of apocalyptic. Sermons on apocalyptic should shine the light of the heavenly reality of the vision on the lives of hearers today. Grenz and Franke articulate the importance of the certainty of this hope: "Biblical hope is always directed toward, anticipates, and draws its life from a particular vision of the future. And the specific future that forms the object of biblical hope is not presented as a possibility, but as a certainty."[14] The grand story of the universe is what God is doing with history through Jesus Christ. The future victory

---

14 Stanley Grenz and John Franke, *Beyond Foundationalism* (Westminster John Knox, 2001), 249. They go on, however, to disparage a hope based on "futurist eschatologies." On the one hand, they rightly criticize an anthropocentric view of eschatology, on the other they sap eschatology of its hope by denying its future orientation.

displayed in canonical apocalyptic texts must become a temporal reality in order for the message to work.

Consider Zechariah's third vision. In it he sees a man measuring the city of Jerusalem, which the angel informs Zechariah will be beyond measure, will have walls of fire, and in which the Lord will dwell with his people (Zech 2:1–13). Why does God give Zechariah this specific vision? Because the people to whom Zechariah was ministering had returned to Jerusalem to find it in ruins. Was *this* the answer to God's promises? They needed a glimpse of the glorious future of God's people to spur their faith in the short run.

That vision is not merely for Zechariah's generation. In Revelation 21:3 John describes his vision of the New Jerusalem: "Then I heard a loud voice from the throne: Look, God's dwelling is with humanity, and he will live with them. They will be his people, and God himself will be with them and will be their God." The vision of God dwelling with his people is ultimately fulfilled in that city. Thus, applying Zechariah's vision to a modern audience can be done by simply updating the means of security:

> Don't we want protection? We do. We have home security systems and car alarms. We pray for safety. But this vision looks far beyond a physical wall. There is no need for a missile shield when Yahweh is your wall of fire. Don't we want satisfaction? We do. We look everywhere for it: money, relationships, achievement, popularity. We seek it through grades, careers, kids, athletics, and retirement. We buy phones and cars and TVs chasing it. Our culture tells us we are valuable in and of ourselves. But deep down we know that we need more. God's glory will be all that we need. It is his greatness that satisfies. While we rebuild, let us keep our eyes on what Jerusalem will be.

Identify Faulty Views of Victory

When offering hope by giving glimpses of the future victory of God, it may be helpful to identify faulty views of victory. These conceptions or expectations could be revealed by studying the context of the original recipients of the vision or the attitudes and beliefs of the modern audience. Identifying faulty views of victory is part of what Bryan Chapell calls discerning the fallen-condition focus of the passage.[15] He explains how a sermon should apply to the lives of the congregation by virtue of the connection between the situation of the original audience of the biblical text and the modern audience. He argues that a sermon faithful to the text in this way "(1) focuses on the fallen condition that necessitated the writing of the passage and (2) uses the text's features to explain how the Holy Spirit addresses that concern then and now."[16]

For example, consider again Zechariah's third vision, addressed to Israel after they return to the land to find Jerusalem in ruins. A faulty view of victory in their circumstances may have been the temporal success of rebuilding the city, the temple, and their homes. In those terms they were not experiencing victory. The vision, however, gives them a greater view of God's victory when the Lord literally dwells with his people: "The declaration of the Lord: 'I myself will be a wall of fire around it, and I will be the glory within it'" (Zech 2:5). For a contemporary audience a faulty view of victory might be limiting it to career success, good health, family success, financial prosperity, etc. Using specific examples of these lesser victories helps listeners see the direct application of the apocalyptic vision to their lives.

Alternatively, take the example of Ezekiel's second vision in Ezekiel 8–11. As he is shown the idolatry in the temple in Jerusalem the intended effects are outrage and mourning. This vision serves to help Israelites in exile in Babylon to process the news that the temple had been destroyed. It is entirely plausible that the first wave of exiles thought: "God would never allow the temple to be destroyed. At least we have that." However, the apocalyptic vision confronts this inadequate view of God's provision. The greater agenda is not the temple, but the spiritual restoration of the people. The key concept here revealing faulty views of victory

---

15 Bryan Chapell, *Christ-Centered Preaching* (Baker Academic, 2005), 48–57.

16 Ibid., 50.

is the premise: "God would never give me cancer or let our church die or let our Christian school go broke...." Guiding listeners to think on these temptations helps connect the passage to their circumstances.

Point to the Just Judge

Sermons on apocalyptic can also offer hope by giving glimpses of God's judgment of the wicked. Keeping in mind that sensitivity is needed when addressing judgment, two fruitful lines of application focus here are warning and comfort. One specific warning in these passages is to believers feeling the heat of persecution who are tempted to give in. Commenting on Revelation 18:4, Robert Mounce observes, "The persecuted church has always faced the temptation to compromise with worldliness and thus ease the tension of living in a hostile environment."[17] An additional warning is to those who reject God's authority. This is one place in sermons on apocalyptic visions where a natural opportunity exists for evangelistic preaching.[18]

The application focus on comfort is a direct result of appreciating the reality of suffering in the lives of the original audience of these visions. In most cases they were on the losing side. Daniel and Ezekiel ministered to Israelites in exile in Babylon. Zechariah spoke to disappointed Israelites who had returned to Jerusalem. John delivered his vision to the first century church facing various levels of Roman persecution. To these first readers, justice must have seemed far away. Apocalyptic literature gave comfort through visions of God adjudicating perfect justice. Even the ironic funeral dirge of Revelation 18 where kings, merchants, etc. mourn the destruction of Babylon is intended to comfort Babylon's enemy: the church. Adela Collins notes that in this case when judgment "is on an enemy, the dirge takes on a paradoxical or ironic character, because of the unlikelihood of genuine mourning."[19] In other words, to the readers it was good news.

---

17 Robert Mounce, *The Book of Revelation,* rev. ed. (Eerdmans, 1997), 327.
18 See Homiletic Strategy 8, "Preach the Gospel," in Chapter 6.
19 Collins, *Crisis and Catharsis,* 120–121.

Sermons on apocalyptic can also point to the just judge by focusing on God's justice for victims of abuse. In Revelation 6:10 the souls of martyred saints cry out, "how long until you judge those who live on the earth and avenge our blood?" It is as if they cry out wondering if their lives and deaths matter, but the seven seals, trumpets, and bowls of John's vision are God's answer to that prayer. This is made explicit in Revelation 19:2 where a great multitude praises God because "he has avenged the blood of his servants that was on her [Babylon's] hands." The vision affirms that believers will be marginalized, but only for a time. This applies to the most extreme instances of persecution as well as the less extreme. Christians may decrease in significance and stature in the eyes of a culture, but rather than grasp for waning power we can be content in the knowledge that the martyrs' prayer will be answered. This line of application is especially relevant in situations where persecution of believers is in the news, or when a cultural shift results in further disaffection of the culture towards the church. Consider taking time in the service to get updates from the church in a closed culture or take time after the sermon to pray for the persecuted church.

In the description of the judgment of Babylon, which stands for godless culture *in toto*, an angel approves of God's judgment for Babylon because "In her was found the blood of prophets and saints, and of all those slaughtered on the earth" (Rev 18:24). The last line is important, because it explains that God's anger with pagan culture is not only because of the killing of Christians, but also because of the unjust killing of anyone for the purpose of Babylon's success. As Richard Bauckham states: "God's judgment of Rome is also attributed to her slaughter of the innocent in general."[20] The future victory of God's people includes righting the wrongs of abuse.

The ultimate vision of God as the just judge is in Revelation 20:11–15. In this scene, all the dead are judged by God and "anyone whose name was not found written in the book of life was thrown into the lake of fire" (Rev 20:15). The finality of this judgment paves the way for enjoyment of the untainted kingdom of God forever. Mounce comments: "With this vision we close

---

20 Richard Bauckham, *The Climax of Prophecy* (T&T Clark, 1993), 350.

forever the chapter on sin and stand ready to enter the eternal state of glory."[21] Interpretive differences on how many judgments to expect do not change the point of the vision. Once again, warning and comfort are appropriate applications.

Identify Faulty Views of Justice

As with the picture of the victory of God's people, presenting God as the just judge who will render his final judgment on the world means faulty views of justice will be exposed. Two potential distortions of God's perfect justice are petty wrath and limiting justice to earthly courts. In both cases apocalyptic visions free listeners to find contentment in God rather than be frustrated by incomplete or inadequate notions of justice.

In Revelation 16 John is shown a vivid image of the wrath of God in the bowl judgments: "Then I heard a loud voice from the temple saying to the seven angels, 'Go and pour out the seven bowls of God's wrath on the earth.'" People are often uncomfortable thinking of the wrath of God. Perhaps unbelieving family members or dear deceased friends come to mind. Note how in a sermon on Revelation 16 Thomas Long confronts this delicate issue directly and explains that discomfort with God's wrath is linked to mistaken notions that his wrath is like human wrath:

> The problem with our understanding of the wrath of God is not that we have made too much of it, but precisely that we have made too little of it. Or, to be more exact, we have conceived of God's wrath in ways that are too small, too interpersonal, too psychological. We have pictured a wrathful God as a larger version of a wrathful us—peeved, petty, and petulant.... To the contrary, though, to speak of God's wrath is to speak of God's liberating and redemptive love pitted against all that opposes it, all that would keep humanity captive and in slavery.[22]

---

21 Mounce, *Revelation*, 374.
22 Thomas Long, "Praying for the Wrath of God," in *Preaching Through the Apocalypse,* ed. Cornish R. Rogers and Joseph R. Jeter Jr. (Chalice, 1992), 137–138.

Note how Long indirectly draws attention to distortions of God's righteous wrath. Listeners can make the connection to their own experiences of petty wrath. Long also helpfully juxtaposes faulty wrath with the real thing. This enables a confrontation to have a helpful tone rather than sounding like harsh condemnation. If you feel listeners need help seeing how they might have a faulty view of God's wrath try using a concrete image. For example:

> Sometimes we unintentionally think of God as a bigger version of ourselves. When someone cuts in front us on the road we speed up and try to do the same to them. But that petty revenge is far from the perfect justice of our holy God.

Another expression of faulty justice is limiting justice to temporal earthly systems. People who have suffered as victims of crime and abuse rightly long for justice here and now. When earthly courts fail, apocalyptic visions point us to the guarantee of justice in the end. The wicked cannot escape the long arm of God's perfect judgment. Acknowledging failures in earthly courts is the first step of offering faith-based hope to victims. The second step is helping them entrust themselves to the perfect judge. In sermons on visions of judgment, consider using a tone of empathy and compassion when addressing victims. Recalling crimes and abuse will be emotionally difficult for listeners. Apocalyptic is not meant to leave people emotionally distraught, but rather to offer genuine hope for real resolution to their suffering.

Call for a Revolution

As sermons on apocalyptic offer hope, they enable the audience to experience a revolution in their interpretation of their circumstances. The other-worldliness of these visions is intended to help people realize that their faith is well-founded even in the midst of persecution and that their perseverance is worth it. Even martyred saints did not lose when they lost their lives. The hope presented in apocalyptic visions proves that they actually win in the end. Jeffrey Arthurs explains that apocalyptic answers believers in crisis "by announcing a competing interpretation of reality, helping the audience change perspective."[23] This new perspective is a revolutionary assessment of suffering, persecution, and marginalization.

In the course of preaching on apocalyptic visions be wary of failing to call people to this revolutionary mindset. It may be appropriate to point out that suffering and persecution are not necessarily signs of God's displeasure. During times of crisis believers will be tempted to compromise, complain, or retreat into despair. Remind listeners that these visions teach us suffering may be a part of God's plan, but it is not permanent. Temporary suffering is not synonymous with losing. Apocalyptic reveals that even if believers suffer, they win in the end. Note this example from a sermon on Revelation 6:9–11 regarding the souls of martyred saints awaiting justice:

> So they were told to rest a little while longer. That word rest says so much. It says those who lost their lives for their faith are not suffering. It says the wrongs they suffered will be made right. It says God's plan is still at work. Why does the church in John's day need to know this? Why do we? Because many days we will fail to see the world in light of the reality of God's sovereignty. Our suffering is not a sign that we are not loved or that God has failed. Even as we face challenging circumstances we need a revolutionary worldview—a worldview in which we rest awaiting the culmination of God's redemptive work. To walk by faith today we must see the world through this lens.

Summary of Homiletical Strategy 7

Apocalyptic visions offer hope to the church. Sermons on these visions should convey this hope by honestly dealing with evil and giving a preview of the victory of God's people and his judgment of the world. Offering hope also involves clearly dealing with faulty conceptions of victory and justice. This hope enables listeners to change their perspective, adopting a revolutionary mindset towards crises.

---

23 Jeffrey D. Arthurs, *Preaching with Variety* (Kregel, 2007), 181.

- Honestly appraise evil and suffering.
- Give glimpses of victory.
- Point to the just judge.
- Call for a revolutionary perspective.

In our preparation to preach apocalyptic we have worked on staying anchored to the text by recognizing the narrative shape and characterization of apocalyptic visions. We learned to pay attention to communication by noting the aural effects of apocalyptic. We focused on following expert guides in interpreting figurative language. In this chapter we highlighted the need to allow apocalyptic literature to transform our perspective on good and evil. In Chapter Six we turn to the issue of context: keeping track of the literary surroundings of apocalyptic visions.

For Further Study

Chapell, Bryan. *Christ-Centered Preaching*. Baker Academic, 2005. 48–57.

Collins, Adela Yarbro. *Crisis and Catharsis: The Power of the Apocalypse*. Westminster, 1984.

Long, Thomas. "Preaching Apocalyptic Literature." *Review and Expositor* 90 (1993): 371–381.

Talk about It

Discuss various ways people struggle with evil. What are reasons many reject an absolute moral standard? What are the different kinds of trials that can cause a crisis of faith?

Dig Deeper

Read Thomas Long's article "Preaching Apocalyptic Literature." In his introduction he compares and contrasts two extreme positions on preaching (or not) biblical apocalyptic literature. Which side of the spectrum do you lean toward? Consider what a healthy approach to preaching apocalyptic might look like in your ministry context.

Practice

Review the concept of the fallen-condition focus on pages 48–57 in Bryan Chapell's *Christ-Centered Preaching*. Assuming you are preaching the vision in Zechariah 5:1–4, identify the fallen condition focus of the original audience and also a modern audience. Highlight two or three key areas of application and brainstorm how you would address them in your sermon.

6

Literary Context of Apocalyptic Visions: Visions as a Part of the Whole

> *...we should note that even the smallest books of the Bible consist of whole discourses. If propositions by themselves were quite sufficient, the Scriptures might be composed of a long list of individual sayings. Instead, God has given us narratives (some quite long), hymns, letters. And these various portions are brought together in a coherent and unified whole. The principle that the Bible is its own best interpreter is not wishful thinking.*[1]
>
> — Moisés Silva

AWARENESS OF THE LITERARY surroundings of a text is essential in preaching apocalyptic (as well as any other genre in the Bible). Successfully catching and casting the vision means being aware of three levels of literary context of a given apocalyptic vision: the immediate context of the biblical book, the message of the biblical book, and the context of the canon of Scripture.

Interpretive Insights

The literary contexts of both the biblical book and the canon warrant careful homiletic attention because they are a direct result of the Spirit producing the Word of God through human authors.

---

[1] Moisés Silva, *God Language and Scripture,* vol. 4 of *Foundations of Contemporary Interpretation* (Zondervan, 1990), 124.

We find both OT and NT apocalyptic visions in texts mixed with other genres. Apocalyptic is one of several sub-genres that together constitute the genre of prophecy, and apocalyptic visions serve a specific purpose in the greater design of the book in which they are recorded.[2] In the OT the natural habitat for apocalyptic visions is prophetic anthologies. Sermons on OT apocalyptic need to be built out of a firm grasp of the argument and organization of the prophetic book. In the NT the apocalyptic vision of Revelation is mixed with the epistolary sections of chapters 2 and 3.[3] Sermons on Revelation need to be crafted with attention to how the book is organized—especially the relationship of the visionary passages to the epistolary section.

Identifying the function of an apocalyptic vision as a subset of a larger prophetic work enables the preacher to connect the dots between the vision and the overall message of the book. David Aune correctly notes that apocalyptic literature "can exist as an independent text or as a constituent part of a host genre, and must be recognized on its own terms in either setting."[4] Recognizing apocalyptic on its own terms means appreciating it as a distinct genre, but that does not mean we neglect to explain how it fits with the text around it.

In addition to their native literary homelands, apocalyptic visions also contribute to the overarching coherence of the canon. If the specific genre traits of apocalyptic are the trees, then the literary context is the forest. Allowing the shape of apocalyptic to shape a sermon means zooming out to consider the function of the vision in both its book and the canon. Probing these two aspects of the literary context of apocalyptic visions is an essential component of sermon preparation.

---

2 While many scholars recognize more sub-genres within prophecy, D. Brent Sandy holds that prophecy is made up of "oracles of salvation, announcements of judgment, and apocalyptic." See D. Brent Sandy, *Plowshares and Pruning Hooks* (InterVarsity, 2002), 107.

3 Some debate whether Revelation is an epistle with apocalyptic or apocalyptic with epistolary sections. Even so, which genre is primary does not change the overall message and homiletic task of seeing how the parts work together.

4 David E. Aune, "The Apocalypse of John and the Problem of Genre," *Semeia* 36 (1986): 80.

Implications of Inspiration—How Does Apocalyptic Fit?

The Holy Spirit inspired not only the content of Biblical apocalyptic texts, but also their final canonical forms. Paying attention both to the literary context of the particular book in which we find apocalyptic as well as the canonical context is an implication of the inspiration of Scripture. Millard Erickson's definition of inspiration highlights that the Holy Spirit worked through human authors to produce the books of the Bible: "By inspiration of Scripture we mean that supernatural influence of the Holy Spirit on the Scripture writers that rendered their writings an accurate record of the revelation or that resulted in what they wrote actually being the Word of God."[5] This definition is based on 2 Peter 1:21 which states that biblical authors "spoke from God as they were carried along by the Holy Spirit."

What about the organization of longer prophetic works like Ezekiel or Revelation? Is the structure of these books also inspired? Michael Grisanti has argued that the Spirit played a direct role in the composition of books of the Bible and the editorial process. With regard to the inspiration of OT books he argues that "the initial composition of a biblical book *and* any editorial revisions of a biblical book before the finalization of the OT canon are part of God-breathed Scripture."[6] While questions of provenance and redaction may interest scholars, what matters to the preacher are questions of the structure and purpose of the final, edited work. The preacher should ask: "How does this vision contribute to the message of its biblical book? Why did the author or editor, under the influence of the Spirit, organize this work in this particular way?"

Preachers will pay attention not only to the context of the book in which the vision is placed, but to the wider context of the whole Bible. This attentiveness to canonical context results from our belief that God has spoken the entirety of the Bible. Bryan Chapell notes the importance in sermon preparation of moving beyond

---

5 Millard Erickson, *Christian Theology,* 3rd ed. (Baker Academic, 2013), 169.

6 Michael Grisanti, "Inspiration, Inerrancy, and the OT Canon: The Place of Textual Updating in an Inerrant View of Scripture," *JETS* 44 (2001): 580, emphasis his.

the literary context of a book to its significance in the canon: "No text exists in isolation from other texts or from the overarching biblical message. Just as historico-grammatical exegesis requires a preacher to consider a text's terms in context, correct theological interpretation requires an expositor to discern how a text's ideas function in the wider biblical message."[7] Here the key question in crafting a sermon on an apocalyptic vision is how it contributes to the message of the canon. What is its relevance to the grand story of the redemption of sinners through Jesus Christ?

Literary Structure Matters

Literary texts are not accidental; the purpose of a text will dictate the parts. Teun Van Dijk has shown that the structure of a text impacts its meaning.[8] The important point he made is that the message of a text controls and influences its semantic organization. Literary texts are formed with comprehensible unity or coherence, and sermons on apocalyptic need to make clear to the audience how a given vision fits. Grant Osborne's concept of the hermeneutical spiral helps the preacher keep in view the relationship of the message of a book to its subunits. He offers three practical steps in this process: "...first, we chart the whole of a book to analyze its flow of thought in preliminary fashion; next, we study each part intensively in order to detect the detailed argumentation; finally, we rework the thought-development of the whole in relation to the parts."[9] Osborne's steps for studying a text help the preacher exegetically navigate the literary context of apocalyptic visions.

Homiletical Strategy 8: Connect the Contextual Dots

Sermons on apocalyptic visions should reflect the message of the entire book and how the vision contributes to it. Having asked

---

7 Bryan Chapell, *Christ-Centered Preaching* (Baker Academic, 2005), 275.

8 Teun A. Van Dijk, *Some Aspects of Text Grammars* (Mouton, 1972), 130, 272.

9 Grant R. Osborne, *The Hermeneutical Spiral* (InterVarsity, 1991), 22–23. While the verbiage here most readily applies to epistles, the format works for studying any genre.

how the inclusion and organization of the material contributes to communicating the message of the book, a sermon on apocalyptic should show the audience how the different pieces of a text fit together to make the whole. Preachers should have a solid grasp of the overall message of the book in which the apocalyptic vision occurs and the immediate literary context of the vision, and they should connect those dots for the congregation. Connect the contextual dots by disclosing the message of the book, and showing how the vision contributes to the message of the book.

Unpack the Immediate Context of the Book

When preaching on apocalyptic visions unpack the immediate context by explaining where the vision fits in the flow of thought in the book. Sermons on apocalyptic should recognize the distinct nature of apocalyptic versus other genres in a text and make clear how it functions in its literary context.[10] If the sermon is part of a larger series through the book, make reference to previous messages and give short summaries throughout the series. If the sermon is a one-time message, then purposefully craft a short explanation of the surrounding literary context.

For example, consider the apocalyptic vision in Isaiah 6:1–13. Isaiah's vision of the throne room of God sits between the song of the vineyard in chapter 5 and the oracle of salvation in chapter 7 given to Ahaz, king of Judah. So how does chapter 6 relate to chapters 5 and 7? John Oswalt argues that chapters 1–5 constitute a general introduction to the failures of Israel and chapters 7–12 home in on specifics.[11] He explains that the vision of chapter 6 "… functions like a hinge, containing as it does words of utter doom and yet the example of the prophet's own cleansing and the concluding note of hope."[12] To connect the dots in a sermon on the vision in Isaiah 6 the preacher might say:

---

10 On the unique structure of Revelation see Stephen Pattemore, "Revelation," in *Discourse Analysis of the New Testament Writings,* ed. Todd Scacewater (Fontes, 2020), 713–744.

11 John Oswalt, *The Book of Isaiah, Chapters 1–39,* NICNT (Eerdmans, 1986), 173–174.

12 Ibid.

Yes, Israel is the unfaithful vineyard of chapter five, but all is not lost. The captivating vision of God's glory results not in judgment, but in atonement. Starting in the next chapter the book of Isaiah will confront much sin in Israel (and in us), but the vision of chapter six prepares sinners to seek refuge in God rather than despair.

Disclose the Message of the Book

In order to connect the contextual dots, we need to know what the dots are by awareness of the unique message of the books in which we find apocalyptic visions. Consider the visions of Ezekiel as a test case. Ezekiel's four apocalyptic visions are spread across his prophetic anthology. The first and last visions serve as complimentary bookends for the book as a whole. In his first vision, he sees God's heavenly throne on the move even while Israel is in exile. In his last vision, he sees Israel restored to her glorious and improved tribal inheritance, complete with a new temple and new geography. These visions work together with the rest of the book as a complete unit. John Hilber summarizes the message of Ezekiel: "Yahweh, the God of glory, must judge his rebellious people, yet he will restore a repentant remnant to covenant blessing in the land, where they will enjoy his glorious presence forever."[13] The last vision pictures that final aspect of the message. Because God is enthroned and sovereign over all the earth, the future of his people and their salvation is secure even though they are in exile.

When preaching Ezekiel's fourth vision allow the context of the book to influence the sermon by connecting the dots of the concluding vision to the starting place of the book. For example:

> It's easy to feel out of place at school or work. Even in our families we can feel a sense of displacement. Our hearts long for a home, and not just any home. God created us to long for him. In the climactic conclusion of Ezekiel's fourth vision, he sees God's people finally restored to the promised land, dwelling with God directly. It's no mistake that this vision culminates in

---
13 John W. Hilber, *Ezekiel* (Cascade, 2019), 3.

the exact opposite of Israel's circumstances in exile in Babylon in the 6th century BC. In the vision, God highlights not only the renewal of the land physically, but also specific land allotments for each tribe. His people have a place, and their place is with him. [PAUSE] We have a place, and our place is with him. As we walk through the end of Ezekiel's last vision, don't miss the significance that God will not only heal the land, but he has designated an inheritance—a piece of the land—for his people. What will happen on this land? He will dwell with his people.[14]

Again, consider Isaiah's vision of God's throne room, but this time in relation to the message of the book. Peter Gentry and Stephen Wellum summarize the overall message of the canonical edition of Isaiah as "the development from corrupt Zion in the old creation to restored Zion in the new creation."[15] If we adopt their summary, or one similar to it, we then need to explain how Isaiah 6:1–13 contributes to that message.

This grand vision not only reveals Isaiah's cleansing by God and his commission to confront old creation Israel, it also offers hope for the new creation. The diagnosis is sober, but the cure is found in the throne room of God. Isaiah's vision of God's glory, his acknowledgment of his sin, and his forgiveness by atonement stand out as the shining light of hope and motivator of repentance and faith throughout the book.

Show How the Vision Contributes to the Message of the Book

The canonical form of Daniel is split roughly in half. The first half is composed of narrative (court tales), and the second half is composed of apocalyptic visions. The first vision in Daniel 7:1–28 coincides with aspects of the dream of Nebuchadnezzar in 2:31–45.

---

14 Interpreters who take Ezekiel's fourth vision to refer to geo-political Israel during the millennium might phrase this slightly differently, but the overall point would not change.

15 Peter J. Gentry and Stephen J. Wellum, *Kingdom through Covenant* (Crossway, 2012), 435.

John Collins argues that this vision is "a transitional chapter, tied to the preceding tales by the use of the Aramaic language and by affinities with ch. 2, but tied to the following visions by its subject matter and by its close parallels with ch. 8."[16] Andrew Hill specifies the unified message in chapters 2 and 7: "Here Daniel's vision of the four creatures and Nebuchadnezzar's statue dream are in concord—after a series of earthly kingdoms God will demonstrate his absolute sovereignty by establishing an eternal and universal kingdom (cf. 2:44)."[17] If the purpose of the book of Daniel is to show the faithfulness of God to Israelites in exile and to call them to live by faith as modeled by Daniel and his friends, then this vision provides a basis to trust God amidst political upheaval.

Connecting the dots for this vision means making clear why the themes of chapter 2 need repeating in visionary form and how they establish the reason for trusting God:

> The chaos is all around us. Politics. Wars. Even the weather seems to defy order and rational explanation. Because so much of our lives just happens to us, it often feels like chaos—an unorganized raging sea whose waves just keep thrashing and pounding. Even the kings and kingdoms we see around us seem to be a product of the chaos—or they at least seem to be contributing to it. Our own government, in what is arguably one of the most advanced and sensible cultures on the planet, often functions like a three-ring circus. What hope is there in such a world? Whether we are looking at the big picture or the minute details of our lives, it's easy to lose hope. The visions of Daniel were given by God for such a time as this. Daniel's first vision picks up on a theme from Daniel 2: God's sovereignty is absolute, and all earthly kingdoms will give way to his kingdom. This truth bears repeating. So, in this chapter they are once again presented to us in visionary form. We need these truths to help us walk by faith as the chaos rages around us.

---

16 John J. Collins, *Daniel with an Introduction to Apocalyptic Literature* (Eerdmans, 1984), 79.

17 Andrew E. Hill, *Daniel*, Expositor's Bible Commentary, rev. ed. (Zondervan, 2008), 143.

Often the best place to connect the dots of the literary context is in the introduction to the sermon, or possibly during a pre-sermon Scripture reading. Zechariah's eight night visions occur at the outset of the book, after a brief call to repentance in Zechariah 1:1–6. Joyce Baldwin suggests that these visions are arranged as a chiasm: "The eight visions follow the pattern a b b c c b b a, with the theological climax in the fourth and fifth."[18] She goes on to point out how these visions link together: "All eight visions are meant to be interpreted as one whole, for each contributes to the total picture of the role of Israel in the new era about to dawn."[19] If the message of Zechariah is that God is trustworthy even after evil has seemingly defeated good, then these visions provide the foundation for trusting God. Note the brief connecting of dots in this introduction to a sermon on Zechariah 1:7–17:

> Sometimes we can't help but be overwhelmed by sin and its devastating effects. People wrong others, they wrong us. We try and fail. We get confused, embarrassed, or shamed. In the midst of such times we often look around and wonder, "What is God doing?" The prophet Zechariah ministered to people in the same kind of situation. They had returned to the land but faced much opposition. They had just finally restarted rebuilding the temple thanks to the prophet Haggai, but as they tried to build they were discouraged by their setbacks and their overall situation. The good news is that God was not content to leave them discouraged. So he sent his prophet Zechariah to give them comfort in an unforgettable way. After calling Israel to repent, he gave Zechariah eight visions to show his people that he is still at work and trustworthy. In the first vision he shows them that he hasn't forgotten their suffering. He hasn't forgotten us either.

The fact that Revelation has not only apocalyptic but also epistolary and prophetic features complicates showing how a given

---

18 Joyce G. Balwin, *Haggai, Zechariah and Malachi*, TOTC (IVP Academic, 1972), 84.
19 Ibid., 98–99.

part of the vision contributes to the message. Greg Beale points out that commentators "...now generally acknowledge that John has utilized the three genres of apocalyptic, prophecy, and epistle in composing the book."[20] We have already noted that apocalyptic visions are a sub-genre within the broader literary world of prophetic literature. Similarly, Beale identifies the significance of the term "apocalypse" in Revelation 1:1 as an allusion to Daniel 2 and concludes: "Revelation is best seen as fitting into the genre of OT prophetic-apocalyptic works, especially that of Ezekiel, Daniel, and Zechariah."[21] Robert Mounce agrees: "The term 'apocalypse' used to denote a literary genre is derived from Rev. 1:1, where it designates the supernatural unveiling of that which is about to take place."[22]

When preaching the smaller chunks of the vision in Revelation the preacher should take into account how the apocalyptic and epistolary sections work together to convey the overall message. For example, a sermon on the judgment of Babylon in Revelation 17–18 needs to articulate how that vision contributes to the purpose or main message of the book as a whole. According to Simon Kistemaker, "The purpose of the Apocalypse is to encourage and comfort believers in their struggle against Satan and his cohorts."[23] A visionary representation of the judgment of pagan culture comforts believers by showing them evil will not escape judgment and encourages them to live by faith in Jesus despite suffering or persecution. In a sermon on this vision Joel Eidsness accomplishes this well:

> Every civilization, every empire, every culture, every political ideology, every false religion will one day be buried beneath the dust of death. Only the city of God and those who people it

---

[20] Beale, *The Book of Revelation*, NIGTC (Eerdmans, 1999), 37.

[21] Ibid., 37. For the view that Revelation is not apocalyptic see Robert Thomas, *Revelation 1–7* (Moody, 1992), 23–29, or F.D. Mazzaferri, *The Genre of the Book of Revelation from a Source-Critical Perspective,* Beihefte zur ZNW 54 (de Gruyter, 1989).

[22] Mounce, *Revelation*, 1.

[23] Simon Kistemaker, *Exposition of the Book of Revelation*, New Testament Commentary 20 (Baker, 2001), 54.

are eternally secure. The images John sees are clear. Life lived for self apart from the lordship of Jesus Christ, though attractive at first sight, will ultimately self destruct. Babylon is not only a seductive mistress; she is a desolate city.[24]

Summary of Homiletical Strategy 8

Preaching apocalyptic visions in light of their literary context means connecting the contextual dots for hearers:

- unpacking the immediate context,
- disclosing the unique message of the host book,
- showing how the vision contributes to the message.

Homiletical Strategy 9: Preach the Gospel

Another way to respect the literary context when crafting sermons on apocalyptic is to preach the gospel from these texts. Show how the text at hand contributes to the overarching narrative of redemption. Preaching that does not account for the message of the canon is in danger of missing the forest for the trees. Allowing the text of an apocalyptic vision to drive the message of a sermon also means asking how that specific vision fits into the larger picture of the canon. How does the text in question relate to the whole of the Scriptures? What does it have to do with the grand story of redemption and the death and resurrection of Jesus?

Most evangelical homileticians agree that we not only preach texts, we preach the gospel from texts. However, there is a significant difference of opinion on how this is done.[25] Bryan Chapell, for example, believes that every sermon should make an explicit move to Christ and redemption. Similarly, Randal Pelton argues that

---

24 Joel Eidsness, "Lament for the City of Man, Revelation 17–18," in *Biblical Sermons*, ed. Haddon Robbinson (Baker, 1989), 249.

25 For example, see Scott M. Gibson and Matthew D. Kim, eds, *Homiletics and Hermeneutics: Four Views on Preaching Today* (Baker Academic, 2018). The primary perspectives at the time of this writing are redemptive-historical, Christiconic, theocentric, and law-gospel. The distinctions between the views are important, but they have more common ground than it may seem.

each text should be preached with explicit acknowledgement of how it fits in the redemptive historical plan of God. Abraham Kuruvilla, a prominent critic of the redemptive-historical approach, agrees that sermons can lead to Christ, but by showing how Christ embodies an aspect of God's will which we, his disciples, are to imitate. Kenneth Langley agrees that we are called to preach the gospel, but that it is the gospel of God, not just of Christ, and embraces more than redemption. Each school of thought will address the canonical relevance of apocalyptic texts differently.

For example, Kuruvilla denies the need to allow the context of the canon to exert significant influence on a sermon. He understands the canonical significance of a given text to be a divine revelation of one aspect of Christ's character which must be imitated by believers. He argues his method is the one that:

> best proclaims the specific thrust of the particular pericope, that best positions each text within the trajectory of the book, that best places the theology of each pericope in the overarching canonical momentum of confirmation to Christ, and not least, that best performs a Christological reading of Scripture—hermeneutically, spiritually, and practically.[26]

He affirms the usefulness of the canon, but only in terms of revealing God's standard for Christlikeness: "Rather we need the complete canon to picture the character of Christ—the One, and the only One, who fully met divine demand; it is through the entire corpus of sixty-six books that we learn what it means to be Christlike, through every pericope in both Testaments."[27] A sermon on apocalyptic built from this perspective will focus heavily on the moral takeaways from the vision, and in OT apocalyptic visions would point to Jesus as the example of obedience.

Kuruvilla's view too narrowly focuses on the results of redemption in obedience and neglects the importance of the revelation

---

26 Abraham Kuruvilla, "Response to Bryan Chapell," in *Homiletics and Hermeneutics*, 33.

27 Abraham Kuruvilla, *Privilege the Text! A Theological Hermeneutic for Preaching* (Moody, 2013), 265.

of how God redeems sinners. Certainly, some apocalyptic visions lend themselves well to such a morally focused homiletic (e.g., Ezekiel's second vision of idolatry in the temple in Jerusalem), but is the canon only a revelation of what God calls Christians to be? The canon as a whole reveals not only what God calls sinners to be, but also how he makes it possible for them to be transformed through redemption.

Ken Langley argues that the theocentric thrust of the canon is the story of redemption, and that story is not limited to the work of Jesus: "God is at the center of the Bible. God is at the heart of redemptive history. He is its main character."[28] Langley helpfully reminds us that the story of redemption is not only the story of the work of the Son, but also of the Father and Spirit. Thus, different apocalyptic visions reveal different aspects of redemption, including ways specific to the persons of the Godhead.

Bryan Chapell notes that keeping the specifics of a passage in view is essential to discerning its biblical theological relevance: "...such discernment examines each text's details and context to disclose our human nature that requires the grace of God's instruction and enabling, as well as to disclose the character of the God who provides such grace, which culminates in the person and work of Christ."[29] In this view the sermon should demonstrate an awareness of where the text sits in relation to the death and resurrection of Jesus. Crucially, this is not "finding Jesus" in every text. Instead, as Randal Pelton argues "It's about explaining how each of these preaching portions makes complete sense only in light of what God-in-Christ-by-the-Spirit has accomplished."[30]

Pelton's approach appropriately balances the specifics of the preaching portion with an awareness of the rest of the canon. Preaching the gospel from apocalyptic visions requires an awareness of biblical theology. In contrast to Kuruvilla's view, recognizing the contribution of a preaching portion of Scripture to the

---

[28] Ken Langley, "Theocentric View," in *Homiletics and Hermeneutics*, 88.

[29] Bryan Chapell, "Response to Abraham Kuruvilla," in *Homiletics and Hermeneutics*, 72.

[30] Randall Pelton, *Preaching with Accuracy* (Kregel, 2014), 120.

overall message of the Bible is not a denial of its meaning in the context of the book.

An important part of this process is knowing where the text falls in the chronology of the Bible. Writing in regard to the use of OT quotations in the NT, Darrell Bock highlights how the chronological sequence of the text is a factor in analyzing the canonical relevance: "But it is important to state that when appealing to the whole of Scripture *an awareness of what is antecedent to the given passage and what is subsequent must be maintained*."[31] Chapell agrees: "Christ-centered preaching rightly understood does not seek to discover where Christ is mentioned in every text but to disclose where every text stands in relation to Christ."[32]

In the case of apocalyptic visions, we find four ways they relate to the ministry of Jesus and the canon of Scripture. First, the vision may directly predict the ministry of the Messiah. Second, the text may reveal the need for redemption through the Messiah's ministry. Third, it may give a visionary representation of the future culmination of God's redemptive plan in judgment and salvation. Fourth, the vision may reveal a heavenly reality or motif in biblical theology which finds its ultimate expression in redemption. Asking in which of these four ways the vision relates to Christ and his redemptive work will create a pathway to preaching the gospel from the vision.

Does this Vision Prophesy about the Messiah?

The first way an apocalyptic vision may connect to the canon is by directly prophesying about the Messiah. Many examples of OT apocalyptic are directly quoted in the NT as referring to Jesus. In Zechariah's vision of the priest Joshua, the Lord explains through the mediator that this vision is all about the Messiah. Joshua and the other priests are a sign, pointing to a future event: God will

---

31 Darrell L. Bock, "Evangelicals and the Use of the Old Testament in the New, Part II," *Bibliotheca Sacra* 142/568 (1985): 310, emphasis his. While the concept of "Christ-centered" preaching is controversial in dispensational circles, Bock expresses a nuanced progressive dispensational hermeneutic that takes into account how a given text of Scripture relates to the canon.

32 Chapell, *Christ-Centered Preaching*, 279.

send his servant, the Branch. Both the titles "Servant" and "Branch" are loaded with Messianic expectation. The "Messiah as God's servant" motif is from Isaiah, specifically in Isaiah 49:7; 50:6; 52:13; 53:4–11. God's servant brings redemption to his people through suffering, guilt, shame, and humiliation. The Branch is described in Jeremiah 23:5 and 33:15 as the descendent from David who will reign as king and bring justice to Israel. A sermon on this vision should make clear that Jesus as the Son of David is the Branch.[33]

Another example of an apocalyptic vision that contains a prophecy of the Messiah is Daniel's first vision. In this vision Daniel sees four beasts rise out of the sea and then their kingdoms give way to the human and divine Son of Man. The vision confronts the wickedness of specific earthly kingdoms as representative of all worldly authority. In a sermon on Daniel 7, Bryan Chapell links the message's purpose to the original audience to his audience while showing the canonical significance of the Messianic reference:

> But what Daniel is saying to his people, of his time and the centuries that follow, is that as awful as it may be—evil may have its day, [here Chapell pauses] God will have the final say. He will judge all the misdeeds of man and he will free his people. We are captives in a strange land, but our God is so great we should trust him. Why trust him? Because he's not just great, he's so good. The goodness is expressed as God is reminding his people he will be faithful to provide the redeemer he always said he would. From the very first pages of Scripture, "I will put enmity between the woman and Satan, between her seed and his seed. He's going to strike the heel of her son, but he—the Son—is going to crush Satan's head." And now God is saying, "I will in fact do it." How will it happen? Look at the expression, verse 13… He's like us, but of divine origin. He comes from the clouds of heaven itself… God is saying I will provide

---

33 That connection may be in Matthew's mind in Matthew 2:23. He might refer to the Hebrew word for "branch" (נֵצֶר) and connect it to the name of Jesus's hometown Nazareth. However, the terms are different enough to be questionable. Another explanation is the link between being a Nazarene and being despised. The prophets did indicate that the Messiah would be despised (e.g., Zech 9–14, Isa 53, Ps 22).

through my Son. This one who is like you, but of heavenly origin, a universal and eternal kingdom, as I promised to David, as I promised to Moses, as I promised to Noah, as I promised to Adam and Eve. I will be faithful.[34]

Does this Vision Reveal the Need for Redemption?

A second way apocalyptic visions fit into the story of redemption is by revealing the need for redemption. In Zechariah's sixth vision he sees a scroll (representing God's law) destroying a house. This image is a picture of God's judgment. In Zechariah 5:34 the Lord specifically identifies theft and false witness as the sins in view, but these may be representative of the law as a whole. The message of the vision is that Israel should not think God's judgment of the nations lets them off the hook for their own sin. The need for redemption on display in this vision is at bare minimum theft and false witness, or perhaps more generally any violation of God's law. A sermon on this vision should focus on exposing hypocrisy and false righteousness. The message of the vision is "this is why we need rescue," not "clean up our act." Indeed, the very next vision reveals the removal of wickedness from Israel, offering hope despite past failure.

Another example of a vision that reveals the need for the Messiah's redeeming work is Ezekiel's tour of idolatry in Jerusalem's temple. In this vision he is shown horrific acts of idolatry occurring in God's temple which results in the dramatic departure of God's presence from the temple. The tragic loss provides a theological foundation to help Israelite exiles in Babylon comprehend news of the destruction of the temple. Specific forms of idolatry are highlighted in the vision, and they provide ample opportunity for specific application in a sermon. The vision also provides a hint of why God exposes this idolatry and judgment. As Ezekiel is instructed to prophesy against Israel, he cries out in anguish: "Will this be the end?" God answers with a promise to preserve a remnant (Ezek 11:16–20). That promise shows the need to reveal

---

34 Bryan Chapell, "Letter from a Babylonian Jail," https://www.bryanchapellsermons.com/sermons/letter-from-a-babylonian-jail/?hilite=%27daniel%27.

idolatry for what it is. A sermon on this vision should focus primarily on idolatry, but it should also provide the canonical link by showing how the need it reveals is ultimately answered. For example:

> Idolatry is incompatible with God's presence. Every generation has to honestly assess the idols of their age, and then firmly reject them. We have to know where the battles are and know why we should fight them. The dramatic departure of God's glory from Jerusalem in Ezekiel's second vision is a sober reminder of the jealousy of God. He wants us to love him above all. He wants us to value him more than anything. He wants us to repent of our idolatry, and worship him alone. God promises here to do just what he has done: to send his Spirit to bring people to repentance and faith. When we read the New Testament, we find out that the Spirit of God dwells within individual Christians. This means that Christians are walking temples. As such, idolatry should be incompatible with us. Isn't that just what the apostle Paul says in 2 Corinthians 6:16, "And what agreement does the temple of God have with idols? For we are the temple of the living God…." God has made a way in Christ for us to be his people by removing our sin. So we say no to our idols, whatever form they might take.

Does this Vision Show God's Judgment or Salvation?

A third way a vision may contribute to the canon is by revealing the judgment of the wicked or salvation of the church. Scenes of judgment in apocalyptic visions satisfy the need established in the canon for justice. Scenes of salvation reveal God's grace and vindicate believers who may have experienced suffering, persecution, and martyrdom. Judgment and salvation are both major biblical themes. A sermon on a vision that reveals judgment preaches the gospel by reminding hearers of the certainty of judgment and also presenting God's grace as the only means of avoiding judgment. A sermon on a vision that reveals salvation preaches the gospel by showing which aspect of the plan of redemption is revealed.

Some visions depict a judgment that anticipates or previews God's future, final judgment. For example, in Zechariah's second vision he is shown four horns (Zech 1:18–21). The horns represent the military nations who have oppressed and scattered Israel. Then he sees four craftsmen coming and he asks what they have come to do. The angelic mediator of the vision answers: "These craftsmen have come to terrify them, to cut off the horns of the nations that raised a horn against the land of Judah to scatter it" (Zech 1:21). This vision is a picture of God's judgment of Israel's enemies. How does this scene of judgment fit into the overall story of the canon? At a bare minimum it reveals a fulfillment of Genesis 12:3, where God promises to curse those nations who hate Israel. What about in the NT? The judgment of Babylon depicted in Revelation 18 picks up this note of God judging pagan nations. Robert Mounce observes "Babylon has always been symbolic of opposition to the advance of the kingdom of God. As it fell in times past, so will it be destroyed in the future."[35] Thus Zechariah's vision shows God will not allow oppressors to escape judgment, and it foreshadows his final word of judgment. Any text in which God's judgment is revealed also provides an opportunity to reflect on his grace. Reflecting on the grace of God in a sermon on Zechariah 1:18–21 should not be the primary point or focus, but it is necessary to connect this scene of judgment with the canon. In this sample from a sermon on Zechariah 1:18–21 the main homiletic message is "God will make wrongs right," but note in this excerpt how the larger story of redemption is kept in view:

> Here we come to a hard but important truth: God's zeal for his people also results in the judgment of sinners. God's special love for his people demands that he judge his enemies. Wrongs will be made right. As they were trying to restart the rebuilding of the temple, Israel needed this encouragement: God will make wrongs right. This reality also encourages us. Discouragement is always the result of sin. People are abusive; they kill, steal, rape, insult, cheat, and deceive. But we need not lose hope, because God will make wrongs right.

---

35 Mounce, *Revelation*, 325.

Before we start sharpening our pitchforks, however, we need to remember that Assyria and Babylon aren't the only enemies of God. The more we think about it, we have to acknowledge that on many days we have been God's enemies. Shouldn't God judge us? The good news is not only that God will make wrongs right, but that he has made a way to make wrongs right and redeem his enemies. The gospel says judgment is not the only fate available for sinners. In Romans 5:10 the apostle Paul tells us that God's enemies are reconciled to him by faith in the death of his Son. So one way or another God's justice is satisfied: sin will be paid for either in judgment or on the cross.

Ezekiel's vision of the dry bones is an example of an apocalyptic vision that reveals God's salvation through or after judgment (Ezek 37:1–14). This vision of salvation finds fulfillment in the work of God building his kingdom, specifically through the Holy Spirit's work since Pentecost. The focus of the vision is on the Spirit of God giving spiritual life to a spiritually dead Israel (Ezek 37:14). This vision has a canonical connection to John 20. In Ezekiel 37:9 Ezekiel was commanded to tell the wind to come and give breath to the corpses in the valley. In John 20:22 Jesus appears to the disciples after his resurrection. In that meeting John tells us: "After saying this, he breathed on them and said, 'Receive the Holy Spirit.'" Jesus's breathing on the disciples is the initial fulfillment of what was pictured in Ezekiel's vision.

In a sermon on this vision, Tim Keller notes this fulfillment and its relevance to the modern audience:

> They [Israel] hadn't escaped physical death. They hadn't escaped the ultimate exile, and therefore there was an even greater return from exile, an even greater escape from death that needed to happen. And it did. You know when it happened? John chapter 20 tells us that the disciples of Jesus were gathered together in the upper room. Three days after he had died he appeared physically in the room and remember what he did? He breathed on them and said, 'Receive the Holy Spirit.' What's that about? It's about Ezekiel! It's Jesus Christ saying, 'I am about to lead the ultimate return from exile. I am about to get

you out of the ultimate problem. I am going give you escape from death itself. If you believe in me I will breathe my Holy Spirit into you, and that means that because I was raised from the dead if you believe in me someday you will be raised from the dead. And there is the ultimate hope.[36]

This vision also provides an excellent opportunity for evangelism in the sermon. When explaining the benefits of the gospel—that by faith in Jesus's death and resurrection sinners can be forgiven, welcomed into God's kingdom, and experience blessing with him forever—consider calling potential unbelievers in the audience to respond with faith. Keller goes on in the same sermon:

> How do you get this hope into you? Wouldn't you like to have this at the center of your life? You've got to hear the truth, you've got to be born again by the Spirit, and you've got to believe the gospel.[37]

The book of Revelation is almost entirely made up of visions of judgment or salvation. Keeping in mind its chronological place in the canon and its future orientation, it naturally provides the climactic fulfillment of God's redemptive promises to judge the wicked and redeem the church. This observation holds true regardless of whether or not the preacher interprets the book from a futurist perspective. From John's point of view what he was shown was future, and his readers would not live to see his vision come to pass. This does not negate its relevance to them or to a contemporary audience.[38] John establishes a direct canonical trajectory by quoting or alluding to a myriad of OT texts (many of them visions). Recalling Bock's point about chronological awareness, in preaching Revelation the canonical question in preaching the gospel is how

---

36 Tim Keller, "The God Who Makes Alive," https://gospelinlife.com/downloads/the-god-who-makes-alive-6173.

37 Ibid.

38 This is not to say how one approaches Revelation will not affect how the text applies. A preterist vs. futurist might see different references for a sign in the vision, but they also might agree in the immediate relevance to hearers.

does the preaching portion connect to what has come before. How is the plan of redemption fulfilled in this part of the vision?

One danger in preaching the gospel in Revelation is to flatten or edit out specific references to Jesus's death as the central component of God's plan of redemption. A sermon by Thomas Troeger illustrates what I mean. Preaching on Revelation 7, he gets some things right but misses the text's emphasis on Christ's sacrificial death. Revelation 7:9–17 is the vision of the multitude who came out of the tribulation. They had "washed their robes and made them white in the blood of the Lamb" (Rev 7:14). Troeger emphasizes the juxtaposition of suffering and the hope of the kingdom of God, but he fails to reference the death and resurrection of Jesus. The closest he comes is in a reference to Christ as our savior:

> Look at the people lost to drugs. "For the Lamb in the midst of the throne will be their shepherd, and he will guide them to springs of living water." Since Christ will guide them, we who claim to follow Christ will point them to our savior.[39]

But the image of Jesus as the Lamb connotes the sacrificial character of his death on behalf of sinners. This is made explicit in verse 14 as these saints had washed themselves white in the blood of the Lamb. To omit any reference to the canonical significance of Jesus's death effectively transforms a glorious application of the death of Christ into a generic statement of hope. Christ is the savior, but how? A sermon on this vision should show how the climactic moment of vindication and relief for suffering saints is a direct result of the Lamb's death and resurrection. Rather than ignoring such a climax, try connecting the benefits of the death of Jesus to times of suffering in the lives of hearers:

> Because of the blood of the Lamb, they are able to stand before the throne of God. By faith in his death and resurrection sinners are made saints. Not only that, they serve him as priests constantly. Sin is no longer an impediment, and regardless of

---

[39] Thomas H. Troeger, "Overhearing Love's Music in a Brutal World," in *The Sermon as Symphony,* Mike Graves (Judson, 1997), 254–255.

what happened to them in the tribulation, they now stand in perfect fellowship with God. The key to this victory and ultimate blessing is the Lamb— the Lamb is the shepherd! He guides to living water, he removes all sorrow. So the end gives meaning to the middle: suffering will cease.

Where do we go for relief and comfort when we suffer? We may turn to drugs or alcohol, to affirmation from people, to medicine, to the government, or even to distraction by entertainment. But the blood of the Lamb is our only lasting refuge. His blood cleanses us from all sin and thus guarantees our place before the throne of God. In the Lamb we are sheltered. The middle may be hard. We may cry today, but we won't cry forever. Why? Because the Lamb is the Shepherd.

Does This Vision Point to an Aspect of Redemption?

Some visions do not directly prophesy of the Messiah or reveal the need for redemption or display God's judgment of evil. Instead, they reveal a heavenly reality or motif which points to a facet of redemption. When preaching on these visions identify the key heavenly feature in focus or the biblical motif and explain how they point to the cause or effects of redemption.

The apocalyptic visions of God's throne room connect to the canon in this way. In Isaiah's vision of God's throne room, God's holiness exposes Isaiah's sinfulness and the sin of his people. John Oswalt describes the canonical significance of this section in Isaiah: "Like the rest of the OT, the earlier chapters of Isaiah have sprinkled through them glimpses of God's grace."[40] In the throne room vision God's grace is evident through the provision of atonement by virtue of a flaming coal from the altar. The sacrificial imagery makes clear that God's grace is mediated through sacrifice. The heavenly reality of God's holiness and provision of atonement points to the means of redemption by virtue of the ultimate sacrifice of Jesus.

---

40 John Oswalt, *The Book of Isaiah, Chapters 1–39,* NICNT (Eerdmans, 1986), 53.

Ezekiel's fourth vision reveals the goal of redemption as God dwelling with his people in the motifs of the temple and inheritance of the promised land (Ezek 40:1–48:35). In this vision he is shown the tribes of Israel restored to a transformed land complete with a brand-new temple. It is an idealized presentation of the promised land, complete with new tribal allotments and a brand-new Jerusalem as its centerpiece. Given to Israel in exile in Babylon, this vision develops the motif of God fulfilling his promises to Abraham's descendants. Although living in exile, they are envisioned as settled in the promised land. Although the temple has been destroyed, they are shown a glorious new temple. The final statement of the book underlines the aspect of redemption in view: "The perimeter of the city will be six miles, and the name of the city from that day on will be The Lord Is There." God's redeeming work will make it possible for him to dwell with his people. The thread of this theme runs throughout the OT, especially in the exodus and temple narratives. It is also described in the epistles as the Spirit of God dwelling in believers. In 1 Corinthians 3:16 the apostle Paul writes: "Don't you yourselves know that you are God's temple and that the Spirit of God lives in you?" Likewise, this thread is woven into John's vision in Revelation. As he is shown the new Jerusalem descending to the new earth he writes: "Then I heard a loud voice from the throne: Look, God's dwelling is with humanity, and he will live with them. They will be his peoples, and God himself will be with them and will be their God" (Rev 21:3).

Note how Charles Spurgeon keys in on the canonical significance of each phase of God dwelling with his people in a sermon on this last statement in Ezekiel:

> And yet there is a special place where God dwells among men, and that is in his church. He has but one — one church, chosen by eternal election, redeemed by precious blood, called out by the Holy Ghost, and quickened into newness of life — this as a whole is the dwelling place of the covenant God. Because God is in this church, therefore the gates of hell shall not prevail against her. «The Lord is there" might be said of the church in all ages....

What is it that makes heaven, with all its supreme delights? Not harps of angels, nor blaze of seraphim; but this one fact, "the Lord is there."

The joy and glory of those divine mansions is that "the Lord is there." Heaven's loftiest peak shines forever in this clear light — The Lord God and the Lamb are the light thereof: "the Lord is there."[41]

Summary of Homiletical Strategy 9

Preaching the gospel in sermons on apocalyptic presents the vision in light of the canonical context. Identify the canonical context by asking does the vision reveal the need for redemption? Does it directly prophesy about the Messiah? Does it show God's judgment or salvation? Does it reveal a heavenly reality or motif which points to an aspect of redemption?

- Reveal the need for redemption.
- Identify prophecies about the Messiah.
- Preview God's judgment or salvation.
- Describe a heavenly reality or motif which points to an aspect of redemption.

Homiletical Strategy 10: Reveal the Eschatology

Preaching apocalyptic in light of its literary context brings to light the need of addressing eschatology in a sermon. Often sermons on apocalyptic literature lean towards one of two extremes: over-emphasizing eschatology or avoiding it altogether. One enemy of appropriately handling eschatology in sermons on apocalyptic is laziness; being clear on eschatology requires extra time and energy to assess the details and appropriately word an explanation. Commit to doing the hard work of preparing to deal with eschatology. As C.S. Lewis pointed out in *Mere Christianity*: "God is no fonder

---

41 C.H. Spurgeon, "Jehovah-Shammah: a Glorious Name for the New Year," *Spurgeon's Sermons,* vol. 37 (Ages Software, 1989), electronic ed.

of intellectual slackers than of any other slackers. If you are thinking of becoming a Christian, I warn you that you are embarking on something which is going to take the whole of you, brains and all."[42] Reveal the eschatology in a sermon on apocalyptic by preaching with humility, aiming for theological clarity, and staying relevant to the text.

Preach with Humility

Humility is a prerequisite for any sermon on any genre of Scripture. Preaching sermons on apocalyptic brings the need for humility front and center. Convey humility in a sermon by articulating the fallibility of the preacher, by respectfully presenting dissenting views, and by acknowledging how important the eschatological position has been in Christianity at large.

Humble preaching acknowledges the fallibility of the preacher. In a rare sermon on Revelation, Spurgeon offered this humble caveat:

> I scarcely consider myself qualified to explain any part of the Book of Revelation, and none of the expositions I have ever seen entice me to attempt the task, for they are mostly occupied with a refutation of all the interpretations which have gone before, and each one seems to be very successful indeed in proving that all the rest know nothing at all about the matter.[43]

His example is worthy of emulating. Perhaps start the sermon by acknowledging the difficulty of the task to the congregation with a tone of dependence of God.

We also convey humility by respectfully presenting dissenting views. After all, preaching is not an exercise in theological showmanship but an exercise of humble service. Note that Spurgeon criticized sermons in his day that were too focused on proving

---

42 C.S. Lewis, *Mere Christianity,* first Touchstone ed. (Simon & Schuster, 1996), 75.

43 C.H. Spurgeon, "How They Conquered the Dragon," *Spurgeon's Sermons,* vol. 21 (Ages Software, 1989), electronic ed.

other preachers wrong on eschatology. Humble preaching on apocalyptic presents alternative eschatological viewpoints with grace, not vitriol. This kind of preaching is not only effective, it helps model to the audience how to treat other Christian traditions graciously. Be wary of targeting or demonizing other traditions or eschatological viewpoints.

Furthermore, we need to acknowledge the importance of our eschatological position (or relative lack of importance) in Christian doctrine as a whole. Humble preaching on apocalyptic honestly calibrates the tone of the sermon to the prominence of the doctrine. Practically, this means discerning peripheral from central doctrines. Using the example of views of the millennium, Benjamin Merkle explains how eschatological humility should be driven by an honest appraisal of the weight of a doctrine and strength of alternative views: "…I'm fairly convinced that my view of the millennium is correct. But I also realize that (1) it is not a central doctrine, (2) it only occurs explicitly in one passage in the Bible (Rev 20:1–10), and (3) solid theologians whom I respect hold to differing views."[44]

Preach with humility by honestly appraising the validity of alternative viewpoints. In sermons on apocalyptic offer gentle correctives to the audience about the topic of the apocalyptic text. For example, on a sermon on Revelation 20 consider using a disclaimer in the introduction:

> Today our text focuses on a well-known and controversial aspect of biblical teaching on the end-times: the millennium. In fact, even though many Christians define their eschatology by their view of the millennium, this is the only passage in Scripture that speaks directly to it. As we walk through this text we will discuss the different interpretive options, but note at the outset that the primary point of Jesus' vindication of the church and victory over Satan are not debated.

Humility is a matter of tone. Using a gentle tone in preaching apocalyptic prevents misunderstanding and misapplication of

---

44 Benjamin L. Merkle, *Discontinuity to Continuity* (Lexham, 2020), 3.

eschatology. Striving for humility does not negate the importance of correlating the details of the preaching portion with the rest of the canon. On the contrary, it communicates that such correlation is difficult, and therefore warrants a lower degree of confidence. Strive for a tone of honesty, fallibility, and pastoral concern. When an apocalyptic vision touches on less prominent eschatological doctrines use softening statements: "While not a major theme in the Bible..." or "Christians hold a variety of positions on this issue."

Aim for Theological Clarity

Sermons on apocalyptic that reveal the eschatology aim for clarity. The well-known adage holds true: a mist in the pulpit yields a fog in the pew. Aim for clarity by accurately articulating your theological perspective and accurately presenting other theological positions. In order to clearly express our eschatological position, we need to understand it. Helpful tools in this regard are systematic theologies, position papers written while in seminary, and church or denominational doctrinal statements. Taking a few minutes in sermon preparation to brush up on the specifics guards against imprecision or confusion in the sermon.

A second area in which to focus on clarity is accurately presenting alternative eschatological viewpoints. Sermons on apocalyptic need not summarize, explain, or even refer to every eschatological position on a particular topic. At the same time, when it is helpful to address an alternative view be sure to have an accurate understanding of the current iteration of it. For instance, many critics of dispensationalism refer to views that were once held but have since been refined or even abandoned. Make use of quality resources like relevant chapters in various systematic theologies or recently published books on various views.[45]

Stay Grounded in the Text

One additional way to reveal eschatology is to stay grounded in the

---

45 C. Marvin Pate, ed., *Four Views on Revelation* (Zondervan, 1998); Merkle, *Discontinuity to Continuity*.

text. Do this by refusing to ignore eschatology. In an overreaction to sermons that are heavy on eschatological content, sometimes preachers ignore eschatology altogether. Beware of belittling eschatology in general. Eschew the tired trope: "Are you a-millennial, pre-millennial, or post-millennial? I'm pan-millennial: it'll all pan out in the end." Using jokes or comments like this can unintentionally cause the audience to doubt the importance of eschatology in general.

If eschatology is not prominent in the passage resist the urge to inject it. Sermons on apocalyptic visions should allow the content of the vision itself to limit what eschatological doctrines to address, if any. Preachers may be tempted to use apocalyptic texts as a springboard to waxing eloquent on the finer points of an eschatological system. Identifying appropriate eschatological implications of a vision is important, but we must be wary of allowing eschatological systems to hijack a sermon on a given text. Resist the urge to turn a sermon into an eschatology lecture. In the past, many congregations were tortured by eschatological charts. Staying relevant to the text means limiting speculation. Be careful not to assign too much importance to speculations about aspects of the vision that are not highlighted in the vision explanation. Letting the text drive the content of the sermon is as much about what is not included in the sermon as what is.

For example, in a sermon on the vision of 70 weeks in Daniel 9:20–27, keep in mind that the various views on the 70th week do not constitute the main focus of the passage. After briefly surveying relevant views, consider re-focusing the audience on the main thrust of the text:

> When people talk about Daniel's 70 weeks, or especially the 70th week, they rarely talk about the atoning sacrifice of the Messiah. Yet we have no doubt that this is the main point of the vision. We want dates and details; all the while God wants us to focus on his mission to save sinners. It's not hard to imagine Israel getting distracted by the date of their possible return to the land, just like we are easily distracted by the little and big details of our lives. But when we pause and zoom out, we see that

the Messiah's mission is the center of God's plan. This means that God dealing with sin was more important than Israel getting back to the land. It means that God dealing with sin is more important than you getting that promotion, or solving that family problem, or never getting sick.

Summary of Homiletical Strategy 10

Revealing the eschatology is a difficult but necessary aspect of preaching apocalyptic in light of the literary context of the canon of Scripture. Hard work in this area of sermon preparation will yield fruit. Reveal the eschatology in sermons on apocalyptic by:

1. preaching with humility,
2. aiming for clarity,
3. staying relevant to the text.

Maintaining awareness of the literary and canonical context of apocalyptic visions equips the preacher to keep the message of the sermon linked to the text. Preachers can shape sermons on apocalyptic in light of the literary context by connecting the dots of the organization of the book, by preaching the gospel as it relates to the vision, and by revealing how the vision contributes to eschatology. When we do so—combined with our previous preparatory work of recognizing the narrative structure and characters, listening for the aural effect, following guides on figurative language, and transforming worldview in light of the vision—we will be equipped to preach with confidence on apocalyptic visions. At this point we have covered all but one key component in catching and casting the vision of biblical apocalyptic. Our final need as we prepare to proclaim these visions is to consider their rhetorical effects.

For Further Study

Carson, D.A. *Scandalous: The Cross and Resurrection of Jesus.* Crossway, 2010. 75–111.

Gibson, Scott M. and Matthew D. Kim, eds. *Homiletics and Hermeneutics: Four Views on Preaching Today*. Baker Academic, 2018.

Merkle, Benjamin L. *Discontinuity to Continuity*. Lexham, 2020.

Pelton, Randall. *Preaching with Accuracy*. Kregel, 2014. 117–156.

Talk about It

Discuss the four views on preaching as expressed in Homiletics and Hermeneutics. Reflect on how the views impact preaching apocalyptic. Which view do you find the most compelling? Why?

Dig Deeper

Read D.A. Carson's sermon "The Strange Triumph of a Slaughtered Lamb" (Chapter Three in his book *Scandalous: The Cross and Resurrection of Jesus*). What stands out to you in how Carson approaches preaching apocalyptic? In what ways are you able or unable to discern his eschatology in the sermon? Discuss the effectiveness of the sermon in relation to the explicit teaching on eschatology. Should he have used more? Less? Do you think he accurately preached the main idea of the passage?

Practice

Examine Revelation 20 and make notes on how you would handle explaining the eschatological content. Identify the main idea of the chapter. Draft a few different ways you might explain differing views on the millennium in the sermon.

7

Rhetorical Effects of Apocalyptic Visions: What's the Point?

> *The Lord, in order to show that, even in that case, there was nothing to prevent him from making room for his kindness, set before the prophet in vision a field covered with dry bones, to which, by the mere power of his word, he in one moment restored life and strength.*[1]
>
> John Calvin

IN OUR MISSION TO catch and cast the vision we have considered the primary genre features—the literary "what" of apocalyptic. We conclude by considering the rhetorical aspect of apocalyptic—the literary "why." Biblical apocalyptic literature has rhetorical purpose, and rhetorical criticism of apocalyptic is the study of how the author seeks to persuade their audience by the vision. Rhetoric asks: What is the author doing with this literary text. What are the author's intended effects on the reader or hearer? Literary features are the tools an author uses for rhetorical ends: to persuade the reader or to produce a specific effect.[2]

In many ways this chapter is the appropriate climax of considering how sermons on apocalyptic visions should be shaped by the

---

1 John Calvin, *Institutes of the Christian Religion,* trans. Henry Beveridge (Hendrickson, 2008), 285.

2 Rhetorical features are not strictly identical with genre features. The former are ways the author seeks to persuade his audience, the latter are literary patterns. As we will see, there will be some overlap. See Greg Carey, "How to Do Things With (Apocalyptic) Words: Rhetorical Dimensions of Apocalyptic Discourse," *Lexington Theological Quarterly* 33.2 (1998): 89–92.

genre. When preaching apocalyptic, being aware of the rhetorical effects of these visions enables the preacher to make appropriate application. Missing this component of preaching apocalyptic could leave hearers missing out on why these remarkable passages matter to them.

Interpretive Insights

Surprisingly, rhetorical analysis of apocalyptic visions has not been a major area of biblical studies. Edith Humphrey explains how separating the study of the anthropological and sociological context of visions from the literary and textual context has unintentionally resulted in a neglect of the rhetorical aspect: "This bifurcation of study into 'anthropology' and 'literary studies' has meant that, until rather recently, vision-reports have seldom been examined for their palpable rhetorical power or in terms of the diverse rhetorical roles that they play in their various literary and social contexts."[3]

Apocalyptic visions are charged with rhetorical power. In studying the rhetorical aspect of apocalyptic visions we are asking how the literary pieces work together to create intended results. Speaking of John's apocalypse, Adela Collins notes how the genre form directly contributes to its persuasive power: "The Apocalypse handles skillfully the hearers' thoughts, attitudes, and feelings by the use of effective symbols and a narrative plot that invites imaginative participation. This combination of effective symbols and artful plot is the key to the power of apocalyptic rhetoric."[4] Each apocalyptic vision is made of literary chunks that work together to impact the audience in a specific way.

Before allowing the rhetoric of apocalyptic texts to influence the sermon we need to identify the most common rhetorical purposes. In the previous six chapters we have considered many of the literary features of apocalyptic and the general circumstances of the original readers. Here we focus on the biblical authors'

---

[3] Edith M. Humphrey, *And I Turned to See the Voice: The Rhetoric of Vision in the New Testament* (Baker Academic, 2007), 19.

[4] Adela Yarbro Collins, *Crisis and Catharsis: The Power of the Apocalypse* (Westminster, 1984), 145.

rhetorical purposes: effects on the hearer. Knowing the rhetorical effects of biblical apocalyptic literature helps inform what our purposes should be as we preach it. Identifying the rhetorical purposes of a text answers the "So what?" question in the exegetical-homiletic process. When we consider biblical apocalyptic texts, we find six common rhetorical goals:

- to awaken and focus the attention of readers or hearers to a particular issue,
- to transform their perspective or worldview,
- to motivate them to persevere in their faith despite suffering,
- to foster worship,
- to provide comfort in trials,
- to call them to repentance.

In analyzing the rhetoric of an apocalyptic vision, remember that many visions achieve multiple rhetorical purposes at once.

Apocalyptic Gets the Attention of the Audience

The first rhetorical goal of apocalyptic is getting the attention of the audience and drawing their focus to a particular issue. This is typically accomplished by a shock and awe strategy. The bold, loud, and fantastic scenes of apocalyptic visions are anything but boring. These wild rides get the attention of the audience because they break the mold of expected communication and storytelling forms. Speaking of how this rhetorical strategy is used in the synoptic gospels, Robert Tannehill says: "Forceful and imaginative language can do its work only if it does not fit into our ordinary interpretive structures."[5] Apocalyptic visions are a bucket of cold water to the spiritually drowsy.

For example, in Revelation 11:15 the auditory features of the vision serve to awaken sleepy readers or hearers: "The seventh angel blew his trumpet, and there were loud voices in heaven saying, 'The kingdom of the world has become the kingdom of our Lord and of his Christ, and he will reign forever and ever.'" In

---
5 Robert C. Tannehill, *The Sword of His Mouth* (Fortress, 1975), 54.

her analysis of Revelation 11–12, Humphrey highlights the attention-getting rhetorical strategy: "Given the promise, the suspense, and announcement, and the auditory jolt, we are predisposed to sit up and take notice: at last, the mystery of God! Nor are we disappointed."[6]

Apocalyptic Transforms Perspective

Another rhetorical goal of apocalyptic is to transform the perspective of the audience. We considered this rhetorical purpose in Chapter Five as it related to apocalyptic visions exposing good and evil. It is worth noting that this revolution in worldview is closely linked to the shocking nature of apocalyptic. For example, one rhetorical effect of apocalyptic may be the necessary re-appraisal of the audience's current circumstances.[7] Leland Ryken explains that worldview transformation is a natural effect of apocalyptic visions:

> Visionary literature, with its arresting strangeness, breaks through our normal way of thinking and shocks us into seeing that things are not as they appear. Visionary writing attacks our ingrained patterns of deep-level thought in an effort to convince us of such things as that the world will not always continue as it now is, that there is something drastically wrong with the status quo, or that reality cannot be confined to the physical world that we perceive with our senses.[8]

John's vision in Revelation, when considered *in toto*, serves to transform first-century Christians' fear of suffering into confidence in God's ultimate plan to deal with evil. As Collins notes: "Feelings of fear and resentment are released by the book's repeated presentations of the destruction of the hearers' enemies...the persecutors are destroyed by divine wrath and the persecuted are exalted to

---

6 Humphrey, *And I Turned to See the Voice*, 157.
7 See Chapter 5 for specific ways to accomplish this in a sermon.
8 Leland Ryken, *How to Read the Bible as Literature* (Zondervan, 1984), 169.

a new, glorious mode of existence."[9] Transforming fear to faith is arguably the primary rhetorical goal of the vision. David deSilva describes how John uses the envisioned future to solidify groups of believers in light of varying challenges:

> He relies on the persuasiveness of the future he presents…to engage the hearers and nurture in them the commitment to respond as he would have them respond to innovation within the group, intimidation outside the group, and potential partnership with those outside the group. This makes for a rhetorical strategy that is sufficiently flexible to address every element within John's diverse audience.[10]

Apocalyptic Comforts the Suffering

A third rhetorical goal of apocalyptic is to provide comfort to the suffering. This goal is present in most biblical apocalyptic visions as they were given to communities of believers suffering to one degree or another. D. Brent Sandy notes how apocalyptic provides comfort: "…the faithful are given new hope that this evil world will eventually come to an end. Apocalyptic is a promise of a new age when God's will *will* be done on earth as it is in heaven."[11]

Apocalyptic Encourages Perseverance

The prophet not only hopes his readers will be comforted; he wants them to hang in there, so a fourth rhetorical goal is to motivate believers to persevere in the midst of suffering and persecution. This perseverance is a function of the revelation contained in the vision. What the prophet sees enables the audience to live by faith, regardless of even the most dire consequences. Sandy explains how this rhetorical dynamic works when he states that apocalyptic

---

[9] Collins, *Crisis and Catharsis*, 154.

[10] David A. deSilva, "Rhetorical Functions of Intertexture in Revelation 14:14–16:21," in *The Intertexture of Apocalyptic Discourse in the New Testament*, ed. Duane F. Watson (Society of Biblical Literature, 2002), 221.

[11] D. Brent Sandy, *Plowshares and Pruning Hooks: Rethinking the Language of Biblical Prophecy and Apocalyptic* (InterVarsity, 2002), 111, emphasis his.

"is a battery charge to increase the saints' resolve. Apocalyptic suggests that if persecution becomes so intense that it results in death, the faithful will be much better off, given what they have to look forward to."[12]

For example, in Zechariah's third night vision he sees a surveyor going to measure Jerusalem. An angel informs the man not to bother because Jerusalem will be too big to measure, and the glory of God will be her walls. Having returned from exile to find Jerusalem in ruins, Zechariah's audience is told by God, via the vision: "I myself will be a wall of fire around it, and I will be the glory within it" (Zech 2:5). One rhetorical goal of the vision is that the returned exiles should persevere despite opposition to the rebuilding of Jerusalem and the temple. Jerusalem's future glory is guaranteed, and that warrants steadfast faith no matter what.

Likewise, Ezekiel's vision of the valley of dry bones (Ezek 37:1–14) offers comfort despite Israel's longer than expected time in exile. Calvin notes how this dynamic is at work in the vision: "The Lord, in order to show that, even in that case, there was nothing to prevent him from making room for his kindness, set before the prophet in vision a field covered with dry bones, to which, by the mere power of his word, he in one moment restored life and strength."[13] Calvin focuses on how this vision shows God's mercy and power in granting spiritual life even though it seemed like they were dead and rotting away in exile.

Apocalyptic Fosters Worship

A fifth goal of apocalyptic visions is to foster worship. Believers may struggle to see the glory of God and value him supremely, especially in times of suffering. They may even wonder if God is enthroned at all. Apocalyptic visions often raise the eyes of a marginalized or suffering community to see God's grandeur. Apocalyptic texts that focus on God enthroned, that reveal his judgment of the wicked, or that reveal his salvation of believers affect the audience by filling their vision with the glory of God. The intent is that their

---

12 Ibid.
13 John Calvin, *Institutes of the Christian Religion*, 285.

hearts will be stirred by such sights, and they will be compelled to exalt God in response.

In Daniel's visions God's faithfulness is put on display despite the abuse of God's people by pagan empires. In uncertain times, God's people can rest assured of his sovereignty. Daniel Block notes how moments of despair occasioned these visions:

> Most apocalyptic writings arose in contexts of great spiritual crisis, when God's people were tempted to despair and wonder who was in control of history or if they would survive the present distress. The intention of apocalyptic is not to chart out God's plan for the future so future generations may draw up calendars but to assure the present generation that—perhaps contrary to appearance—God is still on the throne (cf. Dan. 7:18, 21–22, 27; 8:25; 12:1–4), and that the future is firmly in his hands.[14]

In the epic throne room vision of Revelation 4 and 5 God's authority to judge the earth is on display. The song of praise is not merely meant to be understood, it is to be joined by the audience. As Humphrey notes, the purpose of this vision is not to communicate information, but to evoke worship:

> Yet the most profound effect of the vision is not to drive the reader to theological contemplation, or to the construction of propositions, or to the distillation of a theological 'message'. Worship, that other kind of 'orthodoxy' ('right praise'), presses down on the reader as he or she is swept up into a 'proxy' vision engineered by the rhetorical and literary skill of this unlikely seer…the hymnody serves to interpret the scene as well as to stir the reader.[15]

---

14 Daniel Block, "Preaching Old Testament Apocalyptic to a New Testament Church," *Calvin Theological Journal* 41 (2016): 52.

15 Humphrey, *And I Turned to See the Voice*, 185.

Apocalyptic Calls for Repentance

Finally, a sixth rhetorical goal of apocalyptic is to call the audience to repentance. These visions often focus on the specific sins of compromising faith, idolatry, and apostasy in fear of persecution. Will believers identify with the world to live in comfort, or will they stand firm in the faith despite suffering? Collins identifies this rhetorical purpose in the book of Revelation: "On the deepest level, the Book of Revelation provides a story in and through which the people of God discover who they are and what they are to do."[16]

For example, Zechariah's vision of the scroll that demolishes a house is a dramatic presentation of God's judgment on those who may have temporarily gotten away with theft or bearing false witness. In Zechariah 5:4 the Lord says that judgment "will enter the house of the thief and the house of the one who swears falsely by my name. It will stay inside his house and destroy it along with its timbers and stones." While one rhetorical purpose of this vision may be to comfort the victims of such sin, another is to call those engaged in such practices to repent. Why continue a lifestyle destined for judgment? The drama of the vision is meant to spur the sinner on to repent because of the disastrous consequences of failing to do so.

Homiletical Strategy 11:
Aim for a Similar Rhetorical Effect

Having identified six rhetorical goals, we are almost ready to craft sermons that aim at those same goals. Almost. First, we have to take into account the different rhetorical situations of the first hearers of these apocalyptic visions and our own congregations. Then we can consider how to echo the six possible rhetorical effects of the text.

Compare and contrast rhetorical situations by asking what circumstances were the original readers facing. In light of those circumstances, what situations might arise in contemporary culture

---

16 Adela Yarbro Collins, "Reading the Book of Revelation in the Twentieth Century," *Interpretation* 40.3 (1986): 229.

that the vision addresses? For some visions there will be a one-to-one correspondence. For example, the original readers of Revelation were under threat of persecution, and the contemporary audience may be experiencing the same. For other visions the correspondence will need to be scaled for the audience. Ezekiel's audience was literally in exile, experiencing the destruction of their culture before their very eyes. It is unlikely a contemporary audience is experiencing that degree of suffering. Even so, in other ways they may be experiencing marginalization to a lesser extent.

Having identified the rhetorical strategy and compared the contexts, we then need to aim for the same rhetorical effect. Arthurs has argued that "a sermon's *content* should explain and apply the Word of God as it is found in a biblical text, and a sermon's *form* should unleash the impact of that text."[17] If the rhetorical effect of our passage is to give hope, we need to give hope. If it is to confront sin, we need to confront sin. If it is to encourage the discouraged, we need to encourage. But how? Each of the six rhetorical effects of apocalyptic provides a unique opportunity to mirror those effects for the audience.

Shock and Awe

The shocking images and captivating scenes of apocalyptic visions were designed to capture the attention of the audience. Apocalyptic texts accomplish this through both visual and auditory means; they describe dramatic sights and sounds out of the ordinary experience of people. Echoing the rhetorical effect in this case means crafting a sermon that engages and captivates the attention of the audience. Sermons on apocalyptic should be anything but boring. The subject matter of the text is already there; the question is will the delivery match the shock and awe rhetoric of the text. Francis Grimké's caution against bland preaching in general is doubly appropriate in preaching apocalyptic: "Some preachers are entirely too mechanical in presenting the truth, i.e., they fail to vitalize it,

---

17 Arthurs, *Preaching with Variety,* 13, emphasis his. His chapter on preaching apocalyptic literature (178–199) is very helpful for ideas on how to replicate certain rhetorical effects.

to present it in such a way as to arrest the attention and hold it, in such a way as to excite interest, and move to action. You hear what is being said but feel no interest in it."[18]

Consider the example of Daniel's vision of the four beasts in Daniel 7:1–27. Picturing those beasts emerging from the Mediterranean would have been shocking, akin to watching a movie with high quality special effects. Use vivid imagery to help the audience picture the scene. Consider using a contemporary illustration that parallels the image from the vision. Create tension in the audience by asking why such images would be used in the Bible at all. For example, note in the introduction to this sermon on Daniel 7 the way both contemporary illustrations and tension contribute to capturing the attention of the audience:

> As a matter of fact, what are a lion with eagle's wings, a bear with tusks in its mouth, a four-headed leopard, and a ten-horned beast doing in the Bible at all? Such creatures regularly show up on segments of *Xena, the Warrior Princess* or *Babylon 5*, but they seem out of place in Scripture. Why would anyone include the likes of these in the Bible and, considering all the possible sermon texts in the Bible, why would anyone choose to preach about them?[19]

In this example the television show references are dated, but note how referring to science-fiction and fantasy media helps the audience feel the effect of Daniel's vision. Also note the use of tension. By asking why these images are in the Bible he creates a need in the audience to listen to the rest of the sermon. Capturing the attention of the audience need not be a large part of the sermon, but even briefly used early in the sermon it will help keep the audience engaged.

---

18 Francis James Grimké, *Meditations on Preaching* (Log College Press, 2018), 30.

19 Larry Paul Jones and Jerry L. Sumney, *Preaching Apocalyptic Texts* (Chalice, 1999), 52.

Transform Perspectives

Transform the perspective of the audience by revealing how this vision of an unseen spiritual or heavenly reality should change how they think and live. Aim for this effect by asking how the worldview of the original audience needed to be changed. Were they doubting the faithfulness of God? Were they tempted to turn to pagan deities? Then identify the worldview of the contemporary audience. In what ways might they be doubting the faithfulness of God or turning to idolatry in times of crisis? What connects the circumstances of the original readers to the experience of the contemporary audience?

With this rhetorical effect pay attention to the application of the message of the vision. As Richard Taylor observes:

> The question that believers are most interested in resolving as a result of biblical proclamation is: How should we then live? ... If proclamation is made with such questions in mind, the sermon will avoid becoming a disconnected collection of irrelevant comments on an ancient writing. Instead, it will allow the ancient biblical text to speak clearly to the modern context.[20]

In aiming for a similar effect the sermon addresses not only "How should we then live?" but also "What should we believe?" and "How should we respond in faith?" Transform perspectives by revealing how the message of the vision directly impacts how the contemporary audience should believe, think, and therefore live. In a sermon on Revelation, Mark Dever does just that in his conclusion:

> The message of the book of Revelation is this: the sovereign God is what we're waiting for. We're waiting for him to execute his judgments and yet to save us through the blood of the Lamb and to bring us into his presence forever. Is this what you're waiting for? Is this what you're waiting for in your life? I'm sure there are smaller things you're waiting for... You may

---

20 Richard A. Taylor, *Interpreting Apocalyptic Literature* (Kregel, 2016), 150.

be waiting for this service to get over... You may be waiting for lunch, or waiting for something you'll do on Tuesday... You may be waiting in a larger sense for retirement, or you may be waiting for a check to come. Or there are lots of things you may be waiting for. But at your heart, more than any of those things, is this what you are waiting for... for the sovereign God to execute his judgments and yet to save us through the blood of the Lamb and to bring us into his presence forever? You see, though the future holds many other things, this is the one thing that it holds more than anything else for God's people. The future is not meaningless and anonymous and foreboding; it is for us because it is the future with God. And friend, if you're waiting for anything else, I have to ask you, is your wait worth it?[21]

Provide Comfort in Trials

The rhetorical effect of providing comfort in trials is needed in circumstances in which the audience faces evil in one form or another. Israel in exile faced the consequences of their own sin as well as the sin of Babylon. Once they returned to the land, they still struggled with evil within themselves, as well as persecution from enemies in the land. Christians in Roman Asia Minor in the first century faced flare-ups of persecution, sometimes of unspeakable horror. Facing the realities of sin and evil, the believer may doubt and wonder whether or not these wrongs will ever be made right. The biblical apocalyptic texts answer emphatically: God will settle all scores. Those who refuse to repent and turn to God in faith will be judged.

In order to provide comfort in a sermon on apocalyptic consider in what ways the audience is suffering or potentially may suffer. Apocalyptic images of God's judgment and salvation show the audience that God has not forgotten them. Speak directly to the trials and struggles of the audience. Use specific examples to make the contemporary relevance clear. Consider ways to identify potential

---

[21] Mark Dever, "What Are We Waiting For? The Message of Revelation," https://www.capitolhillbaptist.org/sermon/what-are-we-waiting-for-the-message-of-revelation.

idols in the lives of the audience that may be robbing them of comfort and hope. Tim Keller does this well in a sermon on Ezekiel 37:1–14, the vision of the valley of dry bones. He uses the historical illustration of hope and comfort for those suffering in concentration camps during World War II. Note how he highlights false comfort and hope in the illustration:

> If you had a hope or a meaning in life that suffering and death could take away from you then you were a goner in the death camp. If you lived for money, that money was all taken away from you. If you lived for your family, your family was taken away from you. If you lived for status, well, you know, rich and poor were all thrown together in the same hole and dressed in the same rags.... They didn't have a hope that could overcome death. They had a hope only for this life.[22]

Keller goes on to explain the way the vision shows the Spirit of God giving life. He then applies that truth to the illustration: "There is a hope death camps can't take away from you. That's a hope that nothing can eradicate."[23] When hearers identify that they may be living for money or family or status they have the opportunity to then be truly comforted by the hope of Spirit-breathed life. The illustration that suffering in a concentration camp cannot remove hope effectively invites hearers to find comfort even in their lesser suffering.

Motivate Perseverance

Sermons on apocalyptic motivate perseverance by acknowledging the reality of suffering and presenting the reasons depicted in the vision for forging ahead in faith. This rhetorical effect is different than providing comfort in trials. Comfort calms a heart in despair, pain, or discouragement; perseverance urges the suffering believer to continue to walk in faithfulness to the Lord. Identifying specific

---

22 Tim Keller, "The God Who Makes Alive," https://gospelinlife.com/downloads/the-god-who-makes-alive-6173.
23 Ibid.

reasons for perseverance is the means by which believers are motivated. While the circumstances of modern hearers differ from the original audience, the theological truths revealed in the vision are still relevant.

For example, Zechariah's vision of the eyes of the Lord and the anointed ones (Zech 4:1–14) was addressed to returned exiles who were discouraged in the process of rebuilding Jerusalem. The image of the eyes of the Lord in Zechariah 4:10 symbolizes his sovereignty over all of the earth. His anointed ones are enabled by the Holy Spirit to finish the work. The imagery of the vision is designed to affect the readers by giving them a specific reason to persevere: faith in God's sovereignty and provision. In a sermon on this vision consider using the connection point of discouragement to identify where perseverance is needed in the lives of the audience:

> The eyes of the Lord and the anointed ones remind Israel that God is sovereign even over the rebuilding challenges they were facing. Are you discouraged? Do you feel hopeless, as if God has called you to an undoable task? Are you ready to give up? Don't. The truths so vividly displayed in this vision hold true today. God is still sovereign; his work still continues by his Spirit. When we doubt the success of our endeavors, we have forgotten that we serve a sovereign God. The doctrine of God's knowledge of all is meant to be an encouragement to persevere. Not only does he know what we are going through, his eyes are on us, and his Spirit equips us. In our endeavor as a church to advance the gospel we will face—are facing—trials. We will be tempted to despair, and if the success of the mission depended on us, we should. But it does not. Let us look to our sovereign, omniscient God and find confidence to move forward in faith.

Foster Worship

The rhetorical effect of worship is a natural response to the apocalyptic visions that reveal heaven or the throne room of God. Aim for this effect by calling attention to the specific attributes of God in focus in the vision. Consider ways to help the audience move from the captivity of busyness at work, school, and home to captivation with God's glory. Use explicit calls to worship to help the congregation see these are not merely fascinating parts of the Bible, but they are also invitations to worship. In order to do so the preacher may need to acknowledge the difficulties or distractions that may be inhibiting worship in the lives of the hearers.

The grand vision of heaven in Revelation 4 and 5 illustrates how apocalyptic may create the effect of worship. Humphrey notes how the double hymns found in this vision function as a call to worship for the reader as well. She argues that worship of the Lamb and worship of the One on the throne are not mutually exclusive: "In terms of implicit argument, the hymns direct the hearer/reader to accept and celebrate the worship of the Lamb as a rightful component of the worship of the One on the throne… the acclamations do move the hearer/reader to praise the two major figures with one breath…."[24] In a sermon on Revelation 5:11–14, William Willimon juxtaposes the reality of suffering with the glory of God as revealed in the vision:

> O gentle, hurting, baffled, tearful ones, wherever you languish within the sound of my voice, peer through the bars of your cell, turn your head to catch the light through your hospital window, see the vision and hear the song, sung by hosts in heaven and choirs on earth, "Worthy is the Lamb that was slaughtered!"[25]

Willimon does not explicitly call hearers to worship, although such a call to worship is strongly implied. Whether or not you directly exhort the audience to worship may be a matter of style and personality. One creative way to do so is to insert a catena of passages that magnify the Lord, or consider utilizing a closing song and directly connect the sermon to its content. If a sermon on a vision

---

24 Humphrey, *And I Turned to See the Voice*, 187.
25 William H. Willimon, "Good Show," in *Preaching Through the Apocalypse,* ed. Cornish R. Rogers and Joseph R. Jeter Jr. (Chalice, 1992), 90.

like this does not actually call people to worship, be sure that the implicit exhortation is clear.

Call to Repentance

Sermons on apocalyptic aim for the rhetorical effect of repentance by calling for a return to God with clarity, urgency, and compassion. Jeffrey Arthurs describes this as a call to discipleship: "Apocalyptic rejects moral relativism. Preachers should too. Preachers announce that history is predetermined, and the Lamb *will* win, so we must decide now which side to follow."[26] When preachers call for repentance they encourage the audience to turn away from their own sin. This means clearly encouraging the audience to confess specific areas of sin (those referenced in the vision, if applicable) and exhorting them to turn away from that sin toward Christ. Calling to repentance is often accompanied by a warning. If a hearer is one of the wicked, visions that picture God's judgment are an urgent warning: repent or else. Note the example of Jonathan Edwards in his famous sermon "Sinners in the Hands of an Angry God." After describing the threat of God's judgment in detail he offers God's gracious call:

> And now you have an extraordinary opportunity, a day wherein Christ has thrown the door of mercy wide open, and stands in calling and crying with a loud voice to poor sinners; a day wherein many are flocking to him, and pressing into the kingdom of God.[27]

A common pitfall in sermons that call people to repent is a lack of compassion. It is easy to pound on the pulpit and communicate a less than compassionate stance towards the congregation. Think about specific ways to communicate Christ-like humility, care, and concern while issuing a clear call for repentance. Consider

---

26 Jeffrey Arthurs, *Preaching with Variety* (Kregel, 2007), 192, emphasis his.
27 Jonathan Edwards, "Sinners in the Hands of an Angry God," in *Works of Jonathan Edwards: Volume Two* (The Banner of Truth Trust, 1995), 11, electronic ed.

addressing the audience in terms that emphasize the unity of the church, such as "brothers and sisters." Preach using a soft tone and a slower rate of speech to convey compassion.

Summary of Homiletical Strategy 11

When we are preaching apocalyptic texts, aim for effect by identifying the rhetorical features, considering and comparing the situation of the original audience with our audience, and seeking to preach in light of the rhetorical goals of the text. The most common rhetorical goals of apocalyptic visions are:

- capturing attention via shock and awe,
- transforming perspectives,
- motivating perseverance,
- fostering worship,
- providing comfort,
- calling to repentance.

Homiletical Strategy 12:
Plan Worship Services with Purpose

Our final homiletic strategy deals with the sermon's placement in the liturgy rather than the content of the sermon itself. When preaching apocalyptic, plan worship services with purpose.[28] This strategy addresses how the sermon relates to the rest of the worship service in four specific aspects: tone, relationship to the Scripture reading, music, and prayer.

---

28 This strategy is intended for those who are involved in the planning of services in which they preach. While this is the norm, many times preachers are called to preach outside of their home church or ministry. In such cases it is still wise to be in contact with the host church or ministry regarding service details if possible.

Tone of the Sermon

The tone and feel of a sermon influences the tone and feel of the worship service. Sermons on apocalyptic should match the tone of the text. John Piper helpfully defines the tone of a text: "By 'tone' I mean the *feel* that it has. The *spirit* it emits. The emotional *quality*. The affectional *tenor*. The *mood*."[29] He asserts that each text of Scripture has a unique tone, and therefore that the preacher has a responsibility to faithfully convey that tone in the sermon: "The preacher should embody, not mute, these tones."[30] In sermon preparation ask "How will this text make people feel?"

Some tones specific to apocalyptic are warning, awe, comfort, and resolution. After crafting the structure and content of a sermon on apocalyptic take time to review the sermon's tone. Does it match the tone of the text? In texts that warn, is the warning clear in the sermon? In texts that are filled with awe of God's glory, does the sermon use appropriate verbiage? In texts that give comfort, does the sermon offer hope in both content and delivery? In texts that envision the resolution of the problem of evil, does the sermon provide that satisfactory concluding note?

As the sermon on a specific apocalyptic text reflects the tone, it will necessarily impact the mood of the entire worship service. If the preaching schedule has flexibility in your ministry context, ask whether or not the tone of the text is appropriate to the overall service. While every part of Scripture is God-breathed, it is wise to consider which parts of Scripture are most helpful for specific services. An apocalyptic vision of God's judgment of the wicked may not be the right tonal choice for a sober funeral service or a celebratory resurrection Sunday. If the preaching schedule is not as flexible, be aware of how the tone of the sermon will affect the service as a whole. Consider the example of preaching consecutively through Revelation during a time when a tragedy has occurred in the community. In such circumstances a caveat may be helpful before the sermon: "Today as a community we are shocked by what

---

29 John Piper, *Brothers We Are Not Professionals,* 2nd ed. (B&H, 2013), 121, emphasis his.
30 Ibid.

happened this week. In the midst of such suffering God's speaks to us in his Word. Our passage today gives us a vision that is designed to...." In such circumstances, setting the table with such a caveat will help the congregation connect the tone of the service with the potentially different tone of the sermon.

The Sermon as It Relates to Other Components of the Worship Service

Plan with purpose not only by paying attention to the tone of the sermon, but also to the location of the sermon in relation to the other elements of the worship service. In service planning ask, "How will this sermon affect the mood of the service?" Grimké aptly advises preachers to give thought to the impact of the worship service as the people in attendance will experience it:

> Every service should be a kind of mount of vision—a means of helping the people to see God and to see things from the Divine standpoint—and so be lifted to a higher plane, so be strengthened and fortified for the immediate tasks which may be before them.[31]

Fleshing out his point, consider how the sermon will be experienced in proximity to the other facets of the service. Given the content and tone of both the text and sermon, is it best for the sermon to be the final element of the service? Is it ideal to have a congregational response in singing or prayer after the sermon? These questions lead us to consider where to place a sermon on apocalyptic in relation to three common elements of a worship service: Scripture reading, congregational singing and prayer.[32]

In a service in which Scripture reading is a regular component, plan with purpose what texts of Scripture will be read and when. In some ministry contexts the Scripture reading is the text of the

---

[31] Grimké, *Meditations on Preaching*, 11.

[32] I focus here on weekly elements of most worship services. Other service components worth considering in relation to a sermon on apocalyptic are baptisms, the Lord's table, and testimonies.

sermon itself. Be mindful of longer texts and if necessary select a smaller, key portion of the vision to help the congregation focus on the main idea. In ministry contexts where Scripture reading is not the norm, consider using it as a helpful way to augment or balance the tone of the service. Gary Parrett and Steve Kang suggest balancing a NT passage with an OT reading or vice versa. They advise churches to "complement the sermon text for the day with related readings from the other Testament. If the sermon is based on a New Testament passage, a related passage from the Old Testament can be read as well."[33] In selecting a complementary passage, consider using a different genre that underscores a similar main idea or tone. It may be helpful to use a complementary reading that is quoted or alluded to in the vision text. For example, if the sermon is on Ezekiel 37:1-14 (dry bones animated by the Spirit), consider using John 20:19-22 (Jesus confers the Spirit) for the reading.

Another option is to do the Scripture reading after the sermon and use the reading as an opportunity for response and reflection. Keeping in mind the tone and feel of the sermon, consider how the audience might need to respond to the text. Passages that focus on worship, confession, or faith may be especially relevant in light of the subject matter in apocalyptic texts.

Furthermore, when preaching on apocalyptic we should not only be intentional with what Scripture is read and when, but also how Scripture is read. Jeffrey Arthurs makes a strong argument for an intentional reading of Scripture. He argues: "We convey meaning and mood by how we say printed words. Every instance of communication contains both denotative and connotative meanings, and the reader's voice is the primary tool for getting those meanings across."[34] When reading apocalyptic (or complementary passages), invest some time in planning and practicing how the text of Scripture ought to be read. Reading Scripture well prepares the congregation to think deeply about and be impacted by the Word of God.

---

33 Gary A. Parrett and S. Steve Kang, *Teaching the Faith, Forming the Faithful: A Biblical Vision for Education in the Church* (InterVarsity, 2009), 346.

34 Jeffrey Arthurs, *Devote Yourself to the Public Reading of Scripture* (Kregel, 2012), 91.

Planning with purpose when preaching on apocalyptic also means paying attention to the songs used in the service. Plan with purpose by asking how music can prepare the congregation to hear from or respond to God's Word. Two aspects of music in the service are relevant to preaching: the lyrical content of the songs and the feel. If your ministry context has a music pastor or leader be sure to work with them ahead of time. Give them a heads-up on the tone of the text and sermon. If the sermon will be heavy on warning, encourage using songs that incorporate warning or repentance. Some songs like "O Great God" or "Lord Have Mercy" articulate repentance and offer concrete hope in light of the gospel. Consider adding a closing song of worship or celebration to counterbalance a heavier tone. Songs like "Behold Our God" or "Great Is Thy Faithfulness" provide a great outlet for praise after a sermon with a heavy tone. If the tone of the text is uplifting use songs that do the same. In apocalyptic texts with unresolved tension consider closing the service without a closing song and encouraging the congregation to leave in contemplation.

One final way to plan with purpose when preaching on apocalyptic is to think carefully about how the sermon relates to prayer in the worship service. Prayers in a worship service often aim for the purposes of adoration of God, confession of sin, thanksgiving, and supplication. Compare the tone of the sermon with the potential purpose of the prayer. If one rhetorical purpose of an apocalyptic vision is a call to repentance, consider allowing time for a prayer of repentance in the service. Some traditions make use of several different prayers within the service. In such cases consider how the tone of the vision relates. Perhaps include prayer after the sermon as a response to the text. For example, this prayer was used after a sermon on Revelation 12 focusing on perseverance in spite of Satan's temporary raging against the church:

> God our Father, we pause and acknowledge your sovereign reign over the universe. We confess that often we have cowered in fear at Satan's attack on your church. We confess that often we have been distracted from what matters most, and lost confidence in your kingdom. Lord, help us to believe what we

have read today in Revelation 12. We have seen your sovereignty, your protection of the church, and your faithfulness to complete the plan of redemption through Jesus. Holy Spirit, strengthen our faith and spur us on to perseverance. We thank you that your work can never be thwarted, and we ask that you would remind us of that truth daily. May we honor you as we respond to the various kinds of persecution we may face. Be glorified in us, we pray in Jesus's name, amen.

Summary of Homiletical Strategy 12

Plan with purpose when preaching sermons on apocalyptic by maximizing the impact of the sermon in its placement in the worship service. Give attention to the tone of the sermon and its relationship to:

- scripture reading in the service,
- music in the service,
- prayer in the service.

Consider ways to tailor the other components of the service so that they augment the message of the text and facilitate appropriate congregational response.

Taking note of the rhetorical effects of apocalyptic helps preachers maintain their connection to the real world. After all, these visions were not primarily given to the church to be studied, but to be believed and applied. If we lose sight of the rhetorical goals of apocalyptic, we risk casting the vision with no purpose.

For Further Study

Arthurs, Jeffrey. *Devote Yourself to the Public Reading of Scripture: The Transforming Power of the Well-Spoken Word.* Kregel, 2012.

Humphrey, Edith M. *And I Turned to See the Voice: The Rhetoric of Vision in the New Testament.* Baker Academic, 2007. 151–194.

Fox, Michael. "The Rhetoric of Ezekiel's Vision of the Valley of the Bones." *Hebrew Union College Annual* 51 (1980): 1–15.

Talk about It

Talk about the various ways apocalyptic visions are persuasive. In what ways do people today need spiritual persuasion? What specific circumstances do people face that apocalyptic visions are uniquely suited to address?

Dig Deeper

Read Michael Fox's article on the rhetoric of Ezekiel's third vision. Note how he relates the three rhetorical constituents: strategies, situations, and effects. Identify specific ways to incorporate rhetorical analysis into your exegesis and sermon crafting.

Practice

Examine the apocalyptic vision in Daniel 9:20–27. Identify the rhetorical goals of this vision. How will you reflect the rhetoric of the text in a sermon? List ways to aim for the rhetorical effect for each rhetorical goal you identified.

Conclusion

> *Blessed is the one who reads aloud the words of this prophecy, and blessed are those who hear the words of this prophecy and keep what is written in it, because the time is near.*
>
> Revelation 1:3

WE NEED TO PREACH the apocalyptic visions of the Bible. Preaching apocalyptic is worth the hermeneutic and homiletic hard work because the truths contained in biblical apocalyptic are necessary to sustain the Church until the end; the time is near. As you endeavor to preach apocalyptic, let me encourage you to personal application and homiletic endurance.

For all the difficulty in studying apocalyptic texts and preparing sermons on them, be sure to allow the Word to speak to you. Daniel Block argues that application of apocalyptic to the preacher is central to the task of preaching apocalyptic:

> [A]s with any other type of literature, the authoritative preaching of the message of apocalyptic texts requires on the one hand, that we draw the applications for the present from the main points—rather than engaging in endless speculation about the spiritual significance of details—and on the other, that preachers make the message their own before they declare them to the people.[1]

---

1 Daniel Block, "Preaching Old Testament Apocalyptic to a New Testament Church," *Calvin Theological Journal* 41 (2006): 52.

Preaching is never merely an academic task. The preacher proclaims the Word of God to the people of God as a member of the people of God. Ezekiel and John had to eat the book to proclaim it. It may sound odd, but we need to eat apocalyptic texts to proclaim them. Yes, study them, but also pray through and meditate on them. Apply them to your life and circumstances.

Finally, do not give up. Perhaps we who preach apocalyptic texts need to heed the call to persevere. Frequently in John's vision he encourages the reader to conquer or overcome by faith. In Revelation 21:7 Jesus proclaims: "The one who conquers will inherit these things, and I will be his God, and he will be my son." There are many plausible reasons to avoid or delay preaching biblical apocalyptic texts; it is hard work. Press on by faith! Overcome the challenges and preach this crucial part of God's Word. He is faithful. Reading, preaching, and hearing apocalyptic are a means of blessing to the Church.

Then he said to me, "Don't seal up the words of the prophecy of this book, because the time is near.
Revelation 22:1

Appendix 1: A Philosophy of Preaching

Sermons are like jars of clay: even the best are far from perfect. Even though they bear the flaws of the preacher, God is still pleased to graciously work through humble servants and their earthly efforts. The more I preach, the more I witness confirmation that the Spirit must supernaturally illuminate the Word of God in the hearts of people in spite of our feeble attempts to explain and apply it. There is no formula or process that can guarantee this, apart from actually preaching from the Scriptures.

Even a brief survey of the field of homiletics reveals a plethora of approaches to preaching. Given that this book is a homiletic study, it is only fair to put my cards on the table and communicate my philosophy of preaching in order to help the reader understand my approach to the craft of preaching. Preachers from different backgrounds and ministry contexts with different personalities will preach the same text from the Bible in different ways. Therefore, my philosophy of preaching is not so much a commitment to a particular style of sermon; instead, I aim for eight specific sermon values.

What I Value in Preaching

(1) Rooted in Exposition

An expositional sermon is a sermon in which the main idea of a text of Scripture is the primary point of the sermon, and ideally the sermon would show the congregation how. This is where all the original language, grammar, history, genre awareness, and literary analysis pay off in studying a passage. Mark Dever corrects the often-repeated misunderstanding of expositional preaching as running commentary: "Expositional preaching is not simply producing a verbal commentary on some passage of Scripture. Rather, expositional preaching is preaching that takes for the point of a sermon the point of a particular passage of Scripture."[1]

Expository preaching is also not limited to a particular sermon form (e.g., plural noun propositional sermons, deductive sermons, etc.). As Jeffrey Arthurs notes: "The defining essence of an expository sermon lies primarily in its content, not its form."[2] Two preachers could thus craft two different sermons on a particular text with different outlines and a different wording of the message and yet both be true to the text.

One crucial feature of faithful expositional preaching is limiting the content of the sermon to the preaching portion of Scripture. Charles Simeon articulated this well in his goal for preaching: "My endeavor is to bring out of Scripture what is there, and not to thrust in what I think might be there. I have a great jealousy on this head; never to speak more or less than I believe to be the mind of the Spirit in the passage I am expounding."[3]

(2) Crafted in Light of the Genre

The form, content, and tone of the sermon should be influenced by the genre of the preaching portion. Given the focus of this volume this value should come as no surprise. Specifically, the sermon should not merely teach the truth of the passage; it should do so in a way that takes into account its rhetorical form and purpose. Thomas Long observed that biblical passages are not merely "containers for theological concepts," rather "...they are means of communication."[4]

---

1 Mark Dever, *Nine Marks of a Healthy Church,* 3rd ed. (Crossway, 2013), 44.

2 Jeffrey Arthurs, *Preaching with Variety* (Kregel, 2007), 16.

3 Handley Carr Glyn Moule, *Charles Simeon* (Methuen, 1892), 97.

4 Thomas Long, *Preaching and the Literary Forms of the Bible* (Fortress, 1989), 12.

(3) Informed by Biblical Theology

The sermon's content and main idea should be nuanced in light of the whole of the Scriptures. It is easy to become so focused on the trees in any passage in question that the forest of Scripture is lost. In this I want to be aware of NT-OT connections, as well as the way certain themes are developed in the whole of the canon. David Helm helpfully suggests using four "categories of connections" to discern Biblical theology: prophetic fulfillment, historical trajectory, themes, and analogies.[5] These are not hard-and-fast categories, but they help make clear how a topic in one passage relates to the rest of the canon.

(4) Saturated with Application

A sermon should be infused with specific suggestions and examples of how the passage should be believed, applied, or obeyed. I want never to leave people saying: "That was nice, but what should I do about it?" John Bettler reminds us that preaching *is* application:

> Preaching is driving home the Word of the living God to the lives of His people. It is declaring 'Thus says the Lord' to people who constantly hear other claims for allegiance and direction... Until the preacher has that vision, sees his task in that light, and structures his sermons by that rule, he is not preaching.[6]

(5) Marked by Clarity

The sermon should be easily understandable while not being simplistic. This applies especially to the main idea and related subpoints. If people do not understand the main point, I have missed something. Pierre Marcel argued against using technical language

---

[5] David R. Helm, *Expositional Preaching* (Crossway, 2014), 73–82.
[6] John F. Bettler, "Application," in *The Preacher and Preaching: Reviving the Art*, ed. Samuel T. Logan Jr. (P&R, 1986), 332.

or unnecessary theological rabbit trails in sermons: "In form and language, preaching shall be stripped of everything which does not tend to edify. Superfluous theological discussions, useless or subtle questions which would confuse the believers, are excluded."[7]

(6) Anchored in the Gospel

The sermon should refer to the gospel and seek to explain how the passage relates to the death and resurrection of Jesus. Does it describe why we need redemption? How we are redeemed? Does it flesh out what it means that we are redeemed or the results of redemption? What relevance does this passage have in showing unbelievers the grace of God? I try to include a call to respond to the gospel in each message for those who may be present and do not yet believe. For some passages this is a natural part of the sermon, while in others it takes strategic effort.

(7) Aimed at the Affections

The sermon should target the heart, not merely the intellect, seeking to foster greater love for God, hunger for God, and worship of God. A sermon is not a lecture. The mind may be the gateway to the heart, but merely teaching a text is not the end goal. No one is clearer than Jonathan Edwards on this point: "And the impressing of divine things on the hearts and affections of men, is evidently one great end for which God has ordained, that his word delivered in the Holy Scriptures, should be opened, applied, and set home upon men, in preaching."[8]

(8) Empowered by the Spirit

No matter how the sermon is structured, no matter how creative

---

[7] Pierre C. Marcel, *The Relevance of Preaching*, trans. Rob Roy McGregor, ed. Williams Childs Robinson (Baker, 1963), 79.

[8] Jonathan Edwards, "A Treatise Concerning Religious Affections in Three Parts," in *Works of Jonathan Edwards: Volume One* (Banner of Truth Trust, 1995), 242, electronic ed.

the presentation, if the Spirit of God does not work in the hearts of those who hear, it will not be effective. I agree with Francis Grimké:

> After the most careful and prayerful preparation of a sermon, I am fully persuaded that unless it is used by the Holy Spirit it will accomplish nothing. The endowment from on High is absolutely necessary if results are to follow. The Spirit is needed both in the preparation and in the delivery of the message.[9]

So what can the preacher do? He must recognize his absolute dependence on God for any good to come of the sermon. He must bathe the sermon in prayer and humbly ask for the Holy Spirit's power to draw people to Christ through the sermon, and that each listener's ears, eyes, and heart will be opened to understand, trust, and obey God's Word. As John Piper explains: "Without this demonstration of Spirit and power in our preaching, nothing of any abiding value will be achieved no matter how many people may admire our cogency or enjoy our illustrations or learn from our doctrine."[10]

As I think about these values, I realize that different preachers can accomplish them with very different styles and personalities. I believe that is part of the beauty of God's design for preaching.

---

9 Francis Grimké, *Meditations on Preaching* (Log College Press, 2018), 100.
10 John Piper, *The Supremacy of God in Preaching* (Baker, 1990), 39.

Appendix 2: Sample Sermons on Old Testament Apocalyptic Visions

Sermons are meant to be heard, not read. Reading a sermon rather than hearing it prevents exposure to the inflection of voice, intentional pauses, variation of pace, and even mannerisms and facial expressions that accompany the words. Even so, these sermons apply the principles in this work.

The first sample sermon is by Mitchell L. Chase, who serves as the pastor of Kosmosdale Baptist Church in Louisville, KY, and as an Associate Professor of Biblical Studies at The Southern Baptist Theological Seminary. The second sample sermon is on Zechariah 3—a prophecy about the Messiah. It serves as an example of canonical awareness in preaching apocalyptic.

Explanatory comments in brackets show how the concepts of this study are reflected in the sermons. Scripture is indented for clarity on the distinction between reading the Word, explanation, and application. I have truncated some of the explanation and application for brevity and clarity in publication.[1]

...

---

[1] Refer to Appendix 1 for more on my understanding of the craft of preaching in general.

"Big Trouble from the Little Horn" (Daniel 8:1–27)

Mitchell L. Chase

Opening Hook

The Lord has given you in His Word every reason to trust him. There is no shadow of unfaithfulness, no defect in character, no plan formed in vain, that an honest reader could find. The Lord is altogether righteous, and his ways are perfect. He is exalted above the nations. Any who assemble against him will do so in folly and in failure.

Setting Up Daniel 8

One of the reasons we can trust the Lord is his total sovereignty over history. He is advancing his purposes across time and through empires. No king has risen or fallen apart from the sovereign will of the Lord. When we read the apocalyptic imagery in Daniel 8, we will once again discern textual evidence of divine sovereignty. The Lord makes known the future. And the reason he makes known what is to come is because he has decreed the end from the beginning.

In Daniel 8, the historical context is the reign of Babylon and Israel's exile there. During the reign of King Belshazzar and in approximately 548 BC, the prophet Daniel—now a man likely in his early 70s—had a vision about what was to come. Unlike in the narratives during the first six chapters of the book, Daniel does not understand what he sees in the vision of chapter 8. He needs an interpreter, which will involve an angel named Gabriel—a name we know!—explaining what the vision meant.

The prophet Daniel has learned to trust the Lord in Babylonian exile. The circumstances have not been easy, and the vision will show that tumultuous times lay ahead. But the sovereign Lord of heaven and earth will bring to pass his mysterious purposes through his providence.

The chapter divides nicely in two parts. Daniel's vision is in verses 1–14, and the interpretation of the vision is in verses 15–27.

[Note how Mitchell takes time in the beginning of his sermon not only to introduce the applicational topic of trusting God, but also to introduce the historical context. This applies concepts from Chapters 1 and 7.]

The Vision of a Ram and Goat

Daniel sees a ram standing beside a canal (v. 3). As in apocalyptic visions elsewhere, the appearance of an animal is intriguing and also suggests a meaning beyond a literal animal. (We must await the interpretation section of the chapter to find out the referent here.) The ram has two horns, and with its strength and stamina, the ram charged multiple directions and subdued all the beasts it faced (vv. 3–4). This was no ordinary ram! The track record of this animal meant that its subsequent encounters would probably be intimidating and disastrous for whatever faced it.

Such an encounter is described next, with the imagery of a male goat. A male goat with one horn between its eyes comes from the west, moving with such force and speed that it does not even touch the ground (v. 5). What sort of animal is this? Goats walk—and run—on the ground. So this is no ordinary goat! The goat rushes the ram and conquers it, breaking the ram's horns and trampling it to the ground (vv. 6–7). Suddenly we see that this mighty ram, which seemed so invincible, has now fallen before the even mightier goat.

Daniel's vision then focuses on the victorious goat's single horn. The horn breaks, and replacing it are four other horns (v. 8). And from one of these four horns there comes a "little horn" (v. 9). Something is happening to this goat, and at first the reader cannot tell whether the goat's broken horn is a good result or whether the broken horn means something ominous. As we keep reading, however, we learn that the latter possibility is in fact the case.

Something ominous occurs. This "little horn" grows great, and the direction [where] its strength [was directed] included "toward the glorious land" (v. 9). This land refers to the land of Israel, the promised land. And then we read that its growth meant something negative for the host of heaven. The little horn trampled some of the host of heaven (v. 10). Its power and activity would mean the disruption of sacrifices and the sanctuary (vv. 11–12).

At this point in the vision, the reader would have reason to be concerned about the future for the Israelites. Why? Because we know that the promised land is part of God's covenant with Abraham, and we remember that sacrifices and the sanctuary are rooted in ceremonial commands that are part of God's covenant with Moses. So what is this "little horn," and what does it have to do with the Israelites and their covenants with God? This is a question we want to ask as we look at the final part of the vision and then turn to its interpretation.

One angel asks another angel how long this "transgression that makes desolate" will last (v. 13). The response is "2,300 evenings and mornings," for then the sanctuary and its offerings would be restored (v. 14). The good news is, then, that whatever the "little horn" brings about, the distressing circumstances will be temporary.

[Mitchell explains the symbolic aspect of the text clearly and alerts hearers that the meaning of the symbols will be given later in the text and sermon. This illustrates principles from Chapter 4.]

The Interpretation of the Vision

In the first half of the book of Daniel, the reader was able to see and marvel at how God had gifted the prophet with discernment to understand dreams and visions. Noting this, we might be surprised that this prophet needs an interpreter for the vision he has had (vv. 15–16). In other words, while Daniel can interpret the visions that *others* have, he needs an interpreter for *his own* vision!

The angel Gabriel will help Daniel understand what he has seen (v. 17). The fulfillment of Daniel's vision will take place long after Daniel's own life (vv. 17, 19).

The interpretation begins. Gabriel says that the ram—and its horns—represent the kings of Media and Persia. The Medo-Persian kingdom would be the mighty ram which conquered wherever it seemed to go. In fact, the Israelite exile would come to an end when the Medo-Persian kingdom conquered Babylon in 539 BC! Daniel himself would live through the transition from one empire to the next.

But this seemingly indestructible Medo-Persian kingdom will face trouble—inescapable demise. The goat and its horn represented Greece and its king (v. 21). Though the Medo-Persian kingdom would seem invincible, the goat—Greece—would conquer it. This prophecy was fulfilled in history in 331 BC when Alexander the Great—likely depicted by the great horn between the eyes of the goat—conquered the Medo-Persian kingdom.

Yet Alexander's reign would not last. After his death, his kingdom divided among his four generals. These four generals are the likely fulfillment of the "four horns" that replaced the great horn on the goat. One of the generals, Seleucus, would be followed by the Seleucid line of kings. And in approximately 175 BC, the "little horn" of Daniel 8 rose to power. This was a man named Antiochus IV Epiphanes, a vile Seleucid king who would enact persecution and terror toward the Israelites in the promised land.

Around 167 BC, Antiochus IV aimed his persecutorial power toward Jerusalem. He disrupted the proper worship at the temple when he offered a pagan sacrifice. He forbade Jews from practicing circumcision, and he tried to destroy copies of the Torah. Antiochus tempted Jews with compromise, lest they face his wrath and die a martyr's death.

Antiochus IV Epiphanes was the historical fulfillment of what Gabriel called "a king of bold face" (v. 23) who had great power and caused fearful destruction (v. 24). This Greek king's ways were deceitful, and he pressured Jews to apostatize (v. 25). The host of heaven (v. 10) were apparently the same as the "people who are the saints" (v. 24). Trampling the host of heaven meant persecuting the people of God.

But a group of Jewish men, known as the Maccabees, overcame Antiochus's forces and cleansed the temple, rededicating it for proper worship and sacrifice. This victory in December of 164 BC was marked by a new festival—the Feast of Hanukkah. The horrific experiences under Antiochus IV's reign were temporary—just as the vision had said.

Reaction and Application

Understandably, Daniel was overwhelmed by what he had seen and heard (v. 27). He was literally sick for days. Wouldn't you be distraught if you learned about such terrible things that would come upon your kinsmen? Even though Gabriel had interpreted Daniel's vision, the prophet still didn't understand everything the angel had said (v. 27).

For the prophet Daniel, part of following God faithfully would mean not understanding everything God was doing. And that truth isn't just for Daniel's day. We follow the sovereign Lord of heaven and earth, and he holds all of history in his hand. The ancient rulers of Persia and Greece were under his sovereignty.

Dear believer, there is comfort in trusting our all-wise and righteous God even when we don't understand him. Our lack of understanding doesn't undermine his wisdom or goodness. The fact that his providence is often mysterious doesn't give us any grounds for indignation or accusation toward him. God is good, and his ways are good.

Daniel learned that hard times lay ahead, but the faithfulness of God would be true even in those hard times. The affliction wouldn't last. The circumstances would change because they were changeable. The foundation of Daniel's faith and ours must be the *un*changeable character and promises of God.

The same God who brought Greece against Persia would eventually raise up Rome. And during the Roman Empire, God would give his only-begotten Son. Long after the days of Daniel, and long after the days of Alexander the Great and Antiochus IV, a virgin named Mary would give birth to a son—the promised son, the Lord of lords and King of kings.

The answer to the political and religious tensions in Daniel 8 was not another earthly power, not another military victory, not another ambitious ruler. The answer was the kingdom of heaven which would transcend and outlast all earthly powers.

Though the prophet was sick at the end of Daniel 8, we can rejoice that Daniel 8 was not the end. As part of the larger biblical and redemptive epic of God's plan for sinners, this chapter points

Appendix 2: Sample Sermons on Old Testament Apocalyptic Visions 181

us to the God of Abraham, Isaac, and Jacob, the God who would bring his promises to pass in history.

In a chapter where kingdoms fell and rose, God's people can rightly long for an everlasting kingdom where righteousness and peace shall reign. Only Christ Jesus would fulfill this hope and embody this rule. Only the Lord Jesus would be, for his people, the righteousness and peace they need and desire.

The ultimate solution to the agonies in Daniel 8 is Jesus. The answer to the ram and the goat would be the lamb who put all his enemies under his spotless feet.

[In his conclusion Mitchell helps listeners relate this vision to the rest of the story of the Bible. This illustrates concepts from Chapter 7.]

…

"Wardrobe Change" (Zechariah 3:1–10)

Ryan Boys

There's no denying it, sin makes us dirty. You know the feeling—that spiritual equivalent of having spilled coffee on your shirt. What's even worse is trying to wash it out only to see that your efforts make the stain worse. Now all day you've got a permanent reminder of your fallibility.

Ancient Israel may have felt that way upon their return to Jerusalem from exile in Babylon. Through the prophets God had made it clear that sin was the reason they were in exile, but now they were back. Restored. Everything was going to be different... except it wasn't.

In their attempt to rebuild and restore Jerusalem they had quickly learned that like that coffee stain, sin was still with them. The exile hadn't solved the problem.

Maybe you're feeling that today, feeling dirty because the stain of sin is persistent. Maybe you're struggling with a recurring sin, maybe you're reeling from a new expression of sin, maybe you're just now starting to feel the weight of guilt. The bad news is sin makes us dirty and we are powerless to make ourselves clean. The good news is there is One who can. Let's look at this vision of Zechariah and see God's plan to make us clean.

[In this introduction I front-loaded the application concept of alleviation of guilt due to sin. I also introduced the general context of Zechariah. Before reading the text I briefly introduce the prophet, a concept applied from Chapter 2.]

The prophet Zechariah ministered the word of God to those Israelites who had returned to Jerusalem and kept stubbing their toe on the persistence of their sin. He was given a series of visions revealing particular sin issues in Israel and promises of God for their future. In Zechariah 3 God gives Zechariah a vision of the high priest of his day, Joshua. In verse one we read:

> Then he showed me the high priest Joshua standing before the angel of the Lord, with Satan standing at his right side to accuse him.

In a legal proceeding in the time of the Old Testament the "accuser" would stand to the right of the accused before the judges. The title "Satan" means accuser, and over time it came to be used as the name for the chief enemy of God and tempter of humanity. Here Zechariah sees the accuser doing his worst by accusing the theoretically most holy person in Israel—the high priest. This is exactly what Satan did with Job, and frankly what we often fear.

For many of us it's our worst nightmare: all of our sinful secrets being spilled out before the judge. Satan argues "But they did this. They said this. They thought this." How ashamed would we be? How fearful of judgement? How exposed?

This scene, which is legitimately frightening, begs several questions: What would we say in such circumstances? How would we defend ourselves? What will God do? Look at verse two:

> The Lord said to Satan, "The Lord rebuke you, Satan! May the Lord who has chosen Jerusalem rebuke you! Isn't this man a burning stick snatched from the fire?"

Note how the Lord rebukes Satan, possibly even before the accuser can offer charges! Joshua as the high priest represents the people in the vision. His description as a "stick snatched from the fire" is a metaphor for the nation of Israel rescued from exile. The Lord's point is if he had wanted to destroy his people for their sin, he would have left them in captivity, but they have been rescued. So what about the accusation? Watch what the Lord does in verses three through five.

> Now Joshua was dressed with filthy clothes as he stood before the angel. So the angel of the Lord spoke to those standing before him, "Take off his filthy clothes!" Then he said to him, "See, I have removed your iniquity from you, and I will clothe you with festive robes." Then I said, "Let them put a clean turban on his head." So a clean turban was placed on his head, and they clothed him in garments while the angel of the Lord was standing nearby.

The high priest being described as filthy would have been shocking.

The adjective "filthy" is related to the noun "filth" which refers to excrement or vomit. This is highly unexpected because the high priest usually wore white robes with the ephod—a chest plate with jewels representing the twelve tribes.

[This brief comment on the high priest is an application of helping the audience understand the character from Chapter 2. This explanation could easily be much longer, but I didn't want to get too distracted on explaining the entire Levitical system. Also note that I explained what Joshua represents as a sign in the vision, applying concepts from Chapter 4.]

Maybe the accuser has a point? The people are guilty. But in the vision the angel removes the filthy garments, which represent the sin of the people, and clothes Joshua with a special robe only worn at festival occasions. Why celebrate? God has removed the sin of the people. Rather than stand accused, they should be worshipping in celebration.

This is a clear, powerful picture of God's forgiveness of his people by removing their guilt for sin. Zechariah gets excited and participates in the vision. He calls for the high priest to receive a clean turban as well. This would complete Joshua's glorious uniform, representing his purity after having sin removed. The stain is gone.

The fact is sinners need to be made clean. Like Joshua we need a wardrobe change. The image of God changing the clothes of Joshua the high priest is a powerful picture of his forgiveness. Note that in the vision this cleansing is something done to Joshua, not something that he does for himself.

When we come face to face with the reality of our guilt we often respond in sinful ways. We might deny we are dirty. In our culture today the very existence of "sin" is debated. Or we might feel the guilt of our sin and sink into despair or depression, failing to see the good news of God's saving work. Often, we want to hide from God as if he is waiting for us to make ourselves clean. We might feel like doing good deeds, attending church, cleaning up our act somehow gets the stain out. Deep down we know it doesn't.

If we cannot make ourselves clean, how exactly can we be made clean? Look to verses six through ten.

> Then the angel of the Lord charged Joshua, "This is what the Lord of Armies says: If you walk in my ways and keep my mandates, you will both rule my house and take care of my courts; I will also grant you access among these who are standing here.
>
> "Listen, High Priest Joshua, you and your colleagues sitting before you; indeed, these men are a sign that I am about to bring my servant, the Branch. Notice the stone I have set before Joshua; on that one stone are seven eyes. I will engrave an inscription on it"—this is the declaration of the Lord of Armies—"and I will take away the iniquity of this land in a single day.
>
> "On that day, each of you will invite his neighbor to sit under his vine and fig tree." This is the declaration of the Lord of Armies.

Here God issues a two-fold condition to Joshua and the other priests: if the priests will walk in his ways, then Joshua will rule the temple and have authority over God's courts. He will have the right of access in the rebuilt temple by virtue of God's cleansing work. This is a promise of the restoration of the sacrificial system to Joshua.

Joshua and his priestly colleagues are to listen because they themselves are a sign pointing to something greater: specifically, that God will send his servant, the Branch. Both the terms "Servant" and "Branch" are loaded with Messianic expectation. The Messiah is described as God's servant by the prophet Isaiah. God's servant brings redemption to his people through suffering, guilt, shame, and humiliation. Jeremiah describes the Messiah as the Branch who is a descendent of David who will reign as king and bring justice to Israel.

[The climax of this vision is the explanation by the angel that the changing of Joshua's clothes points to the ministry of the Messiah. Keeping this as the high point of the sermon is an application of Chapter 1, identifying the narrative structure and keeping the main idea of the vision the main idea of the sermon.]

The stone with seven eyes continues to explain the significance of the Branch. This stone is not a precious gem, but rather some kind of large stone for engraving. It is "set before" Joshua—not on his person. This stone represents the temple building. The seven "eyes" represent the Lord watching over the building of the temple (the stone, cf. Zech 4:10b). This stone could very well be the capstone or cornerstone of the temple.

The ministry of the Branch is linked to the temple and its meaning is made clear in Zechariah 6:12. The Branch brings greater forgiveness than even the temple can offer: permanent. Through this Branch, God will remove the sin of the land in "one day."

Given the Servant/Branch connection and the relevant passages in Isaiah, that day must be the day of the Messiah's sacrificial death for sinners. When their sin has been removed they will invite their neighbor to enjoy the abundance of the crops they enjoy in the land. Sitting "under" a vine or tree indicates security and prosperity. Grapes and figs indicate agricultural blessing.

[This explanation of the titles "Servant" and "Branch" is an application of the concept from Chapter 6 of keeping the canonical context in view.]

Sin may make us dirty, but the Messiah makes us clean. The entire priestly office is a sign, pointing forward to the once for all sacrifice of the Servant, the Branch. This is how sinners can be made clean. The author of Hebrews makes this clear in Hebrews 10:10 when he says "...we have been sanctified through the offering of the body of Jesus Christ once for all time."

The exchange of filthy clothes for clean clothes is one of the clearest articulations of the means of forgiveness in the OT. It truly is good news. The Messiah's mission has always been about making sinners clean. The exchange of the guilt of sin for righteousness is a transaction that only the Branch can complete. Once for all, it was done. So we have peace with God.

Are you still stained with sin? Have you been washed clean? Do you have peace with God? Familiarity with the gospel and the experience of grace are not the same thing. If you've never felt clean, felt the burden of guilt lifted, felt at peace with God, then perhaps you are still trying to make yourself clean.

The message of the Bible is not "Make yourself clean." It is "Trust the Messiah, Jesus and he will make you clean." How? By fulfilling the function of the temple forever, by making a once for all sacrifice for sin. There's even more good news. Because of the

Branch we don't have to deny or justify our sin. We don't have to retreat into despair. We certainly don't have to clean ourselves. We are free to confess our sin with full confidence of our forgiveness.

If you're here today and you've never repented of your sin and put your faith in Jesus then your clothes are dirty. I invite you to accept his offer of salvation by trusting in his death on your behalf and his resurrection. He came to make us clean.

[This passage lends itself well to evangelism in preaching, a concept from Chapter 6. I saved it for the end to allow time for reflection and response after the sermon.]

We can't stop Satan from reminding us of our sin, but we can control how we respond. We should take some practical advice from Martin Luther in 1543:

> Jesus Christ certainly did not inspire the thought that the devil will get you; for he died in order that those who belong to the devil might be free from him. Therefore act like this: Spit at the devil and say, "If I have sinned, well, then, I have sinned, and I am sorry about it; but Christ has taken away all the sins of all the world if only people will confess them… and believe in Christ. Therefore this sin of mine is certainly also taken away. Depart from me, devil. I am forgiven."

Sin may make us dirty, but the Messiah makes us clean.

Appendix 3: Sample Sermons on New Testament Apocalyptic Visions

THE FIRST SAMPLE SERMON from the NT is on Revelation 19:11–21 by Lucas O'Neill. Lucas serves as the pastor of Christian Fellowship Church in Itasca, IL, and recently served as an Associate Professor of Homiletics at Trinity Evangelical Divinity School where he taught the concepts communicated in his book *Preaching to Be Heard* (Lexham, 2019). The second is from Revelation 12 and illustrates one way to deal with eschatology in a sermon on apocalyptic.

...

"Vengeance and Vindication" (Revelation 19:11–21)

Lucas O'Neill

We often have a rather sanitized view of Christ. From paintings of a rosy-cheeked shepherd with perfectly parted hair to a skateboarding savior with a sparkling smile, it's hard to imagine Jesus as anything other than calm, cool, caring. Jesus is tender to be sure—he is the good shepherd, he lays his life down for his friends. He looks on the lost with compassion and without his grace none could be saved. But this is too flat an image if we view him as only kind with no severe edges.

Jesus is a good shepherd but he's also a good *king*; he cares and he consoles but he also *conquers*. We're going to turn to a passage of Scripture this morning that serves as a word-picture of who Jesus is. Its words are intended to craft a sort of portrait of Christ in your mind and your heart—not a realistic painting but more surreal. But real nonetheless. Let's let Scripture shape our view of Jesus, however stark its contrast with our current presumptions about Christ.

Turn with me to Revelation 19. Here we have a vision given to John and John's words here are conveying the vision, the painting if you will. The symbols seem weird at first, but it's not a photograph or actual footage, it's more like an imaginative rendering. What it's communicating about Jesus is real but how it's communicating it is through fantastic imagery meant to say more than another genre of literature might allow. If a picture is worth a thousand words, then a surreal painting is worth much more. Now, this image might shock us a bit. But keep in mind John's whole revelation is meant to encourage local churches to face adversity with hope and courage. So let's be ready to receive Jesus for all of who he is because all of it is right and good and perfect.

[Note how O'Neill illustrates concepts from Chapter 4 as he introduces the theme of the text as well as the concept of a vision in the introduction.]

Let's look just at verse 11 to start with. Right out of the gate the vision begins with the understanding that this portrait of Christ, jolting as it may be, fulfils the perfection of who he is.

Then I saw heaven opened, and behold, a white horse! The one sitting on it is called Faithful and True, and in righteousness he judges and makes war. This new vision, beginning with "I saw," opens right away with the claim that Jesus will justly deliver God's vengeance against his enemies. Look at the bold, fearsome portrayal of Jesus—this pure rider on a white horse is descending from heaven and he judges and makes war. Jesus is not a pacifist. But he's pure. Already this disturbs some of our categories. The imagery is going to get hot but first we're told, however gritty the vision gets, Christ's warring judgment is out of his *faithfulness* and *truthfulness*. His warring judgment is in *righteousness*. So, he rides a white horse because he is pure of judgment as we see in chapter 14 when he rides a white cloud or when he sits upon a white throne in chapter 20. It's not wrong for Jesus to judge his enemies severely; it would be impure of him not to. The true ruler of the earth cannot allow wickedness to persist.

Now, where are we in all of this? Listen: for those in Christ, this is a message of hope! We need this because Jesus' delivery of God's vengeance will vindicate the saints. We need to know we have a Savior who sees the troubles of his Bride, the Church, and will step in to end all oppression and wickedness. Let's look carefully at verses 12–16.

His eyes are like a flame of fire, and on his head are many diadems, and he has a name written that no one knows but himself. He is clothed in a robe dipped in blood, and the name by which he is called is The Word of God. And the armies of heaven, arrayed in fine linen, white and pure, were following him on white horses. From his mouth comes a sharp sword with which to strike down the nations, and he will rule them with a rod of iron. He will tread the winepress of the fury of the wrath of God the Almighty. On his robe and on his thigh he has a name written, King of kings and Lord of lords.

His fiery eyes and many diadems speak to his judgment and rule. But believers in Christ don't need to fear his fiery gaze as unbelievers do. Of course, Christ's flaming eyes judge our works, love and faith as John described back in 2:18–19 and 23 in the message to Thyatira. But here, Christ's blazing stare is not on his saints but on his enemies.

There is a way to see this a little more clearly that makes sense of the details we just read in 12–16. Sometimes authors use literary patterns to emphasize their message. What we have in these verses is referred to as a "chiasm"—you can think of it like a sort of sandwich with layers that match each other and the meat in the middle. Check this out on the screen:

   A. *(12) the unknown written name*
      B. *(13a) blood-soaked garment*
         C. *(13b) "Word of God"*
            D. *(14) saints vindicated by Christ's judgment*
         C'. *(15a) sword proceeding from the mouth of Christ*
      B'. *(15b) he treads the winepress*
   A'. *(16) the known name written*

Now, it's not always true that this sandwich pattern is intended to bring heightened attention to the middle piece but it's often true and I think that's what's going on here. Again, John is delivering this revelation to embattled Christians surrounded by persecution and this passage is meant to encourage them, to fortify them. This doesn't put us at the center of the stage; clearly Jesus is the focus here. But it does orient us to where we are in the whole event—Jesus fights not against us but against his enemies who are also our oppressors. Let's make some brief observations about each of these sandwich items, from the outside ends working our way toward the middle.

First, we see that the bread of the sandwich, the bookends if you will, is a focus on the name of Jesus. In verse 12 it is unknown but in verse 16 it is known. He's already been called Faithful and True, and he's referred to as the Word of God in 13. Then King of Kings and Lord of lords—this name is written both on his robe and on his thigh. Perhaps the nations don't know his name as such, but they will now! And, of course, the saints already know him as Lord. Jesus is coming as an unrecognized King, but now fully establishing his reign without room for any disregard as to his proper title. All of the names and titles in this scene stack up to emphasize Jesus' total reign and authority here.

Now look at the next symbol. His garment is blood-soaked in 13a—why? Because he treads the winepress of wrath as described in 15b. As with most of Revelation, the symbols make best sense with the Old Testament as the backdrop. John's not inventing new symbols so much as he's showing Christ's fulfillment of old symbols. Isaiah 63:1–3 carries this same concept: the man marching in strength and treading on his enemies gets his garment soaked in blood as one would trampling grapes in a winepress. It's a gory image that communicates the absolute destruction of God's enemies. God's people have been waiting for what seems an eternity for the Lord's final justice. Revelation reveals that it is Jesus who will do it. How does he do it? That's what's interesting about the next symbol.

Christ's enemies, the oppressors of the saints, are cut down by the word of his mouth which pronounces and fulfills. Since Jesus is the Word of God in v. 13 he strikes down the enemy nations with the word of his mouth in v. 15. The vision is not one of Jesus clanging his sword against shields and armor, but that his victorious word of judgment is undefeatable. How long would this "battle" really take when there are no tenable shields? He smashes them to bits with the rod of iron from Psalm 2. They are just fragile pottery before him.

Now we see this middle piece about the armies of heaven, dressed in pure white linen following King Jesus on their own white horses. I don't think there's any need to see this as an actual fighting element since there is no real resistance to the utter destruction doled out by Jesus' pronouncement. But it does say "armies" so they follow their Lord as his contingent so to speak. They could be angels I suppose, but in John's revelation white garments are almost always applied to the saints. There is one exception to this (15:6), but it is clearly believers in, for those of you taking notes, 3:4–5, 18; 4:4; 6:11; 7:9, 13–14. It's not crucial to make the decision here but, on the whole, it fits that Jesus leads the saints who have been longing for justice against the nations who persecute them as we see in chapters 6 and 7. Jesus shatters the nations but blesses those who take refuge in him as promised in Psalm 2. In Revelation 17:14 John tells us that as the Lamb conquers his enemies, those who are with him are the called, chosen and faithful.

So, this violent portrait of Christ carries real hope for the Christian. Our garments are made pure by Christ's perfect sacrifice because Jesus took the severe, faithful and true judgment upon himself on our behalf to the glory of the Father. And for that we will bless the Lord always. And we will see the destruction of those who hate Christ and all who ride against him.

[O'Neill not only explains the warfare imagery of the vision but makes specific application to the lives of the hearers—illustrating principles from Chapter 5.]

Now, look: Christ's wrath is a missing category for many of us, but *we should hope in it.* Consider a story I heard in a seminary class. The professor was a professional counselor who specialized in working with victims of abuse. He would provide counselees with Scripture to read and contemplate. A particular client came to him one day, excited that she finally found a verse in Scripture that brought her comfort.

"Which passage is that?" the professor asked. She said, "You know that passage where Jesus comes in riding a horse, wielding a sword, and he cuts down all his wicked foes?" "Yes..." he replied. "*That* one. That passage comforts me, because it means *God doesn't let them get away with it.*"

For those of us dealing with special pain—not just the regular aches of living in a fallen world but the real misery brought on by evil tormentors—God is not oblivious and he doesn't just sweep it under some rug. He's not ignoring it. He's biding his time.

[In this illustration O'Neill applies concepts from Chapter 5, directly showing how the vision transforms our worldview in the midst of significant suffering.]

Most of us live rather comfortable lives, so it's hard to get in tune with this verse or that counselor's client. But this is especially comforting to Christians who suffer at the hands of persecutors. The horrific accounts of Christian persecution we can refer to are myriad. Think for instance of the 120 Christians killed in Nigeria by Fulani militants on June 23, 2018, as they were returning from a funeral.[1] The persecution there persists making Nigeria #7 on *Open Doors'* watchlist.[2] Violence against Christians is spiking in India as one news source reported 300 attacks in just the first nine months of last year. Reports include smashed church signage, wrecked sound equipment, and severe beatings.[3] According to *Christianity Today's* annual report: "Every day, 13 Christians worldwide are killed because of their faith. Every day, 12 churches or Christian buildings are attacked. And every day, 12 Christians are unjustly arrested or imprisoned, and another 5 are abducted."[4]

This is why we see the martyred saints longing for Christ's judgment in Rev. 6:10. God doesn't say "vengeance is wrong," but "vengeance is *mine*" (Deut. 32:35). The judgment of Christ doesn't make John think, "Whoa, Jesus I hope this never happens," but rather, he invites the reader to say, "Come Lord Jesus!" (22:20)

This vision allows us to see not simply that Jesus will address the wicked or merely do *something* about it. But he is Faithful and True and will mete out perfect, total justice. No matter the injustice we now face, God will hold the wicked accountable *completely*. We can rest assured that Jesus' vengeance against his enemies will be total. Read verses 17–21 with me—the vision turns to a big feast that confirms the utter totality of Christ's judgment.

Then I saw an angel standing in the sun, and with a loud voice he called to all the birds that fly directly overhead, "Come, gather for the great supper of God, to eat the flesh of kings, the flesh of captains, the flesh of mighty men, the flesh of horses and their riders, and the flesh of all men, both free and slave, both small and great." And I saw the beast and the kings of the earth with

---

[1] "Pastor: 120 Nigerian Christians killed leaving funeral," https://www.baptistpress.com/resource-library/news/pastor-120-nigerian-christians-killed-leaving-funeral.

[2] "The World Watch List," https://www.opendoorsusa.org/christian-persecution/world-watch-list.

[3] "Why India is witnessing spike in attacks on Christians, churches," https://www.aljazeera.com/news/2021/12/2/india-christians-church-hindu-groups-bjp-conversion.

[4] "The 50 Countries Where It's Most Dangerous to Follow Jesus in 2021," https://www.christianitytoday.com/news/2021/january/christian-persecution-2021-countries-open-doors-watch-list.html.

their armies gathered to make war against him who was sitting on the horse and against his army. And the beast was captured, and with it the false prophet who in its presence had done the signs by which he deceived those who had received the mark of the beast and those who worshiped its image. These two were thrown alive into the lake of fire that burns with sulfur. And the rest were slain by the sword that came from the mouth of him who was sitting on the horse, and all the birds were gorged with their flesh.

This is a different feast scene than we saw in verses 6–10. That feast was one of celebration and enjoyment. This is one of judgment and recompense. It might feel new, but in Scripture we often see a feast motif paired with the theme of the outcasts of God's kingdom. The beauty of a fellowship meal contrasted with the casting out of enemies and traitors.

You might recall that at *the Lord's Supper* Jesus promised to eat with his disciples again in the Father's kingdom. This is juxtaposed with Judas' exit in Matthew 26:29. The disciples are promised a meal, the betrayer is promised destruction. In the *Parable of the Ten Virgins*, the door is shut to the marriage feast and the foolish virgins are outcasts (Matt. 25:10). Earlier, in the *Parable of the Wedding Feast*, the usurpers are killed in the King's anger, and the uninvited are cast into outer darkness for weeping and gnashing of teeth (Matt 22:1–13). There's something about feasts in the Bible that refer not just to those who get to enjoy it but to those who are outcasts from it.

John's readers might be reminded of Isaiah 25:6–12 where we see "a feast of rich food." Then it says in verse 9:

It will be said on that day, "Behold, this is our God; we have waited for him, that he might save us. This is the Lord; we have waited for him; let us be glad and rejoice in his salvation."

At this feast in Isaiah, the Lord saves his people and brings down their enemies. So, they wait for him to do it. John is saying, "I see this feast and it truly does bring utter destruction to the Lord's foes. We will be saved from all wickedness, totally." Part of the joy of the feast is the fulfillment of the longing for justice. The first feast in Revelation 19 is one of celebration that the wicked do not get to be a part of. The second feast in Revelation 19 is one where the wicked are the meal. They don't just get left out of glory, they get the full weight of God's wrath.

As Psalm 2 describes, the Son takes on the raging nations and he absolutely crushes them. They are "bird food" meaning they are cursed by God (as we see in Deut. 28). They're utterly destroyed. *All* the birds (17, 21) are called to gorge themselves on the flesh of *all* Christ's enemies—the kings, the captains, the mighty men, the cavalry, the free, the slave, the small, the great (18). They are destroyed from top to bottom, from the greatest to the least. Even the leaders behind it all, the diabolical instigators leading the charge—they are put down finally. The beast and false prophet who deceived the nations face eternal judgment (19–20). Jesus' judgment is perfect and utterly complete. He rides his horse and wields his sword with no competition, no negotiation, and no partiality (21).

[In this section O'Neill references three key biblical passages that relate to this section of Revelation. This is a fine example of making the canonical context clear from Chapter 7.]

The wicked oppose Christ because they would rather worship something or someone else. Some do this knowingly, some do it because they're deceived. But they all make war on the real Messiah, the one who is Faithful and True. But they will not prevail, even if it looks like they have small victories now.

If you're listening and you've not come to grips with where you stand before Christ, you need to understand: you are either with him or against him (Matt. 12:30). This doesn't mean you are as wicked as persecutors who attack Christians, but you do not want to be on the wrong side of things when this feast goes down. You might be the least among them, but wrathful judgment is coming.

"Why do Christians get a pass" you might ask? "Christians aren't perfect" you might say. And you're right. God doesn't simply forget about justice and turn a blind eye for believers. No, Jesus took on flesh to be the perfect worshipers that we all fail to be. Then he took on death, a death he didn't deserve but we do. You'll remember he wasn't killed swiftly or painlessly; He endured wrath and suffering. Christians don't get a free pass that gets them out of judgement. But they place faith in Jesus the Christ who paid for the pass and bore the penalty for our failure. Do you want in? Repent and believe the good news that Jesus lived, died and rose again to conquer death for all those who would call upon his name. Today, you can know you are on the right side of this day of judgment. Call upon Christ the faithful and true savior before you meet him as Christ the faithful and true judge.

Christian, this passage is directly for you. You should be encouraged to persevere even when surrounded by evil, by opposition. Even when enemies of Christ make you their target. They don't hate you, they hate Jesus. We hope and pray that we can steer many of them to repentance through kindness, non-retaliation and gospel witness. Vengeance is not our job. But that doesn't mean we don't long for the day when wickedness will be put away. When Christ will vindicate all of his suffering saints with his perfect and total judgment upon his enemies.

In the end, we get to feast in peace because the enemy is consumed in wrath. Our peace is total because their judgment is complete. Christ's salvation is not only to rescue you out of judgment but to rightly exact judgment on those who rise against him and his own. We can endure evil because we can trust Jesus—he is faithful and true to his word about the judgment he will bring. Rest in the hope of Christ. Our vindication is sure because Jesus' vengeance is total.

...

Appendix 3: Sample Sermons on New Testament Apocalyptic Visions

"We Are at War" (Revelation 12:1–17)

Ryan Boys

Why must we suffer? Throughout the book of Revelation God has been telling the church, through the apostle John, to be ready to suffer and to beware of compromise with our culture. He has called us to be ready to die, if necessary. The entire book presupposes a time of great suffering for the church—present and especially future. But why must we suffer?

This is a powerful question, and one that has driven Western culture from incredible optimism about humanity's ability to rectify evil to a cold, indifferent acknowledgment: evil exists. There is no grand story or purpose for it. It just happens. So when the Islamic fundamentalist beheads a Christian or when the cancer cells can't be stopped, we simply shrug our shoulders and say "Sometimes things just happen."

What if they don't "just happen"? What if everything that happens *is* part of a greater narrative, a grand story of the universe? What if there really is a struggle between good and evil that is beyond us and yet impacts us? It was the Apostle Paul who said: "For we do not wrestle against flesh and blood, but against the rulers, against the authorities, against the cosmic powers over this present darkness, against the spiritual forces of evil in the heavenly places."

Tonight, we will learn from Revelation 12 that we are at war. Make no mistake. Sometimes we forget it. Other times we are all too aware that we have an enemy who is crafty, deceitful, and angry. Find your way to Revelation 12:1–17, and together we'll learn about where the suffering of the church comes from and why we have hope in the midst of it.

[This introduction steers the application to the corporate struggle of the Church, rather than focusing on an individual reading. This application starter is a result of concepts from Chapter 7, thinking through the rhetorical goals of the passage.]

As we came through Revelation chapter 11, we are anticipating the final judgment, but there are more interludes to come. Some scholars call Revelation 12–14 the seven signs in delay before John is shown the seven bowls of judgment. We will walk through these seven signs together, recognizing that some of these signs summarize big chunks of history while others look to the future.

We read in Revelation 12:1–2:

> A great sign appeared in heaven: a woman clothed with the sun, with the moon under her feet and a crown of twelve stars on her head. She was pregnant and cried out in labor and agony as she was about to give birth.

In apocalyptic literature the messenger, here John, is given symbolic visions. Here the vision is described as a sign, meaning what it pictures represents something else.

[Note the use here of concepts from Chapter 4: I explain the concept of signs in apocalyptic literature and go on to explain the significance of the signs in the vision. There is no easy way around this.]

First, we are told about a pregnant woman crowned with twelve stars, shining with celestial light. The woman represents Eve, the mother of humanity. The context includes references to Genesis 3 with a serpent, and the conflict between the seed of Eve and the serpent. The sun and moon imagery is meant to communicate her glory as the mother of humanity. The twelve stars are probably representative of the twelve tribes of Israel. The idea is that from Eve comes the messianic community—both those looking forward to the Messiah, Israel, and those who would believe in him after his arrival, the church. In Isaiah 66:7–9 Israel is depicted as a mother, giving birth to the Messiah. This is exactly what we see happening in the vision. The Messiah—the good guy—is about to be born. If we have a good guy, we need a bad guy. Look to Revelation 12:3–4.

> Then another sign appeared in heaven: There was a great fiery red dragon having seven heads and ten horns, and on its heads were seven crowns. Its tail swept away a third of the stars in heaven and hurled them to the earth.

The woman is about to give birth, and then we see this dragon. Virtually every ancient near eastern culture had some kind of mythology about serpents. There's a Canaanite tale about a seven-headed serpent, just like we have here. In ancient Greek mythology there's a story about a python who tries to kill Apollo before he's born—very similar to what we see here. The Spirit gives John this vision as a play on the serpent theme, and as a corrective. This is really what's going on with the serpent.

You'll notice this dragon has seven heads and ten horns. The ten horns are a reference to the book of Daniel, where the horns are rulers. We're not sure about whether each head has seven diadems or [if] there's one for each head. One way or another, he has a mighty tail that sweeps down a third of the stars of heaven. The stars are either angels who fell with Satan (there may be some connection here with Daniel again), or they're just stars. In either case, the point of the image is to communicate the power of the dragon. We've now met the bad guy. Look next at what he is trying to do at the end of verse 4:

> And the dragon stood in front of the woman who was about to give birth, so that when she did give birth it might devour her child.

This is like a horror movie. A giant red dragon wants to eat this newborn baby. The image is grotesque. The baby is the Messiah, and the dragon is his enemy. Note verses five and six:

> She gave birth to a Son, a male who is going to rule all nations with an iron rod. Her child was caught up to God and to his throne. The woman fled into the wilderness, where she had a place prepared by God, to be nourished there for 1,260 days.

She gives birth to the child, and then John quotes from Psalm 2:9, a messianic psalm. Verse 5 describes Jesus' birth. We have no reference to his life or ministry, only a reference to his ascension. This is a brief summary of the Messiah's ministry. He's born, and goes safely to heaven. The dragon doesn't get him.

While the Messiah was safe, the woman had to flee into the wilderness. Because of the Exodus of Israel in the Old Testament, the wilderness is both a place of spiritual intimacy with God and a place of trial and testing. The two often go hand in hand. She is protected by God from the dragon in the wilderness for three and a half years. That time frame comes from the book of Daniel, and probably indicates a short period of trial and testing. Let's pause right here.

[Using concepts from Chapter 4, I don't make a big deal of the number of days, but I do try to explain briefly that that period of time is linked to Daniel as a time of testing.]

Part of the benefit of apocalyptic revelations is they are hard to forget. This is a vivid vision! The dragon tries to eat the baby, and the baby ascends to heaven and the mother flees to the wilderness. We will find out shortly that the dragon is, of course, Satan. This vision depicts Satan raging against the work of the Messiah. Satan tried to thwart Jesus' ministry is several ways. The primary allusion is probably to the slaughter of the innocents from Matthew. Satan also tempted Jesus after his baptism, and incited Judas into betraying Jesus which resulted in his crucifixion. Satan was constantly trying to undo the work of Jesus and thwart his mission.

[Here I apply concepts from Chapters 2 and 6 in summarizing a few key aspects of Satan in the Bible. Because he is a key character in the vision, it is worth the time to make sure everyone is clear on the details.]

This may not be new information, but too often we forget about this conflict. It's not just a past conflict, it's a present conflict. Satan hates Jesus and the church. Here the curtain is pulled back on the ancient spiritual struggle still ongoing. Our challenge is we live in America and enjoy religious freedom. We might be tempted to forget that Satan hates us and Jesus and is actively seeking to destroy Jesus's work. Though we are at peace, we are not at peace. Don't assume that because we have freedom of religion (for now) that Satan will leave us alone.

This puts the context of our suffering in the light of a much greater spiritual reality. This is a panned-out view of the epic conflict between good and evil. There's an epic conflict playing out right now. The question still remains: why is Satan so active against the Messiah and his church? We see the answer in the next part of the text. Look to verse seven.

> Then war broke out in heaven: Michael and his angels fought against the dragon. The dragon and his angels also fought, but he could not prevail, and there was no place for them in heaven any longer. So the great dragon was thrown out—the ancient serpent, who is called the devil and Satan, the one who deceives the whole world. He was thrown to earth, and his angels with him.

Is this a vision of a past battle in heaven, is it a future battle that will happen at the end times, or is it a symbolic battle representing Satan's defeat by virtue of the cross? I think it's the latter, but the point doesn't change much either way. The key truth is that Satan has lost and yet is currently active on earth. He is called here "that ancient serpent" which is a direct link to Genesis 3. He is also called the accuser and the deceiver of the whole world. This is the nature of Satan's warfare.

[Note how I try to avoid overconfidence in the eschatological detail of identifying to what Satan's defeat refers. This concept from Chapter 6 leads to once again trying to stay focused on the main idea of the vision.]

Michael and his angelic army defeat Satan, and heaven rejoices in verses 10–12:

> Then I heard a loud voice in heaven say, "The salvation and the power and the kingdom of our God and the authority of his Christ have now come, because the accuser of our brothers and sisters, who accuses them before our God day and night, has been thrown down. They conquered him by the blood of the Lamb and by the word of their testimony; for they did not love their lives to the point of death. Therefore rejoice, you heavens, and you who dwell in them! Woe to the earth and the sea, because the devil has come down to you with great fury, because he knows his time is short.

Probably the martyrs in heaven are singing this song of worship and victory due to the victory over Satan through the blood of the Lamb. The Lamb imagery is ironic. The Lamb is not the symbol of a warrior, but of a sacrifice. The dragon comes with power and strength trying to destroy the Messiah. The Messiah defeats him not by strength, but by humility and a sacrificial death. This is the core idea of the vision. Our victory over Satan is through the Lamb. Also, our victory does not come through power or might, but through humble faith and witness— even to the point of martyrdom. Satan, sin, evil, rebellion against God, these are all defeated in the cross of Christ. This victory, however, does not mean that the rest of our days are without suffering.

[This is the climax of the vision, therefore the climax of the sermon as well. Tracing the structure of the vision's narrative makes the climax clear (Chapter 1).]

Note Revelation 12:13-14:

> When the dragon saw that he had been thrown down to the earth, he persecuted the woman who had given birth to the male child. The woman was given two wings of a great eagle, so that she could fly from the serpent's presence to her place in the wilderness, where she was nourished for a time, times, and half a time.

The woman also represents the believing community—both Jews and Gentiles—the church. The woman's eagle's wings is an allusion to the Exodus as God rescued Israel and bore them out of Egypt on eagle's wings. The time frame, whether it is literal or symbolic, indicates that Satan's rage against the church is for a limited time only. He has already been defeated.

Note verses 15-18:

> From his mouth the serpent spewed water like a river flowing after the woman, to sweep her away with a flood. But the earth helped the woman. The earth opened its mouth and swallowed up the river that the dragon had spewed from his mouth. So the dragon was furious with the woman and went off to wage war against the rest of her offspring—those who keep the commands of God and hold firmly to the testimony about Jesus. The dragon stood on the sand of the sea.

Believers in Jesus are the descendants of the woman. That's you and me. We are in this text. Satan will try and destroy the church, but he cannot be successful. Nature itself joins the fight, symbolizing God's protection of the Church against Satan's attacks. Our victory over Satan by the Lamb means his rage is in vain. After the cross, Satan's rage intensified. Yet his rage is futile.

As we see in passages like 2 Corinthians 10:3–6 and Ephesians 6:10–20, Satan attacks our faith, our beliefs, and our worldview. He wants us to refuse to believe that he exists, and that he is raging. But the vision reveals Satan exists, and while he is a finite being, he and his demons are on the offensive all around us, raging against God's church. Our victory over Satan by the Lamb means his rage is in vain. We may suffer his attacks, but he cannot defeat us. We may even die, but because of the Lamb we are still victorious. Therefore, we as the Church need to be ready to endure Satan's attacks.

[In this section I applied concepts from Chapter 5 by explaining how the truth of the vision transforms our worldview. In this case the focus is on potential suffering of the Church.]

Back in World War II, Operation Overlord was the Allied offensive that began with [the] Normandy landings. Once Operation Overlord had begun, the war was on the way to conclusion. Germany would be defeated a year later.

Even so, it would be within that year that the allies would suffer their greatest number of casualties. Although the Germans were effectively defeated by the fall of 1944, in December they launched a major counter-offensive in Belgium, France, and Luxembourg. The allies were caught off guard, and their lines "bulged" eastward, hence the title "Battle of the Bulge." This counter offensive was defeated, and yet it showed how careful the allies had to be.

When we suffer and when we are persecuted, we need to remember that it is part of the grand story of history. Christ has defeated Satan; our role is to walk by faith regardless of his raging. The church's victory is secure. Our victory over Satan by the Lamb means his rage is in vain.

Appendix 4: Summary of Apocalyptic Hermeneutical Insights and Homiletic Strategies

	Hermeneutic Insights	Homiletic Strategies
Apocalyptic as Narrative	Apocalyptic texts contain a vision report in a first-person narrative. In the vision a prophet or apostle is taken on a visionary journey and tells the story of that journey.	#1- Tell the Story
		#2- Divide the Text Appropriately
Apocalyptic Characterization	The revelation is given to a prophet and explained by an "other-worldly being" (usually an angel, but sometimes God himself).	#3- Invite Hearers to Journey with the Prophet
Apocalyptic Acoustics	These texts were read aloud, and therefore often use literary devices that target the ears of the hearer.	#4- Echo the Aural Effect
Apocalyptic Signs and Symbols	These visions make use of signs, symbols, figurative characters, and numbers. Some of these may be intentionally bizarre and shocking to the reader.	#5- Paint the Picture
		#6- Follow the Vision Interpreter
Apocalyptic Transcendent Visions	Apocalyptic reveals the transcendent reality of the ultimate salvation of God's people and/or the reality of heaven in a vision. Often this will include a clear delineation of good and evil, and a focus on the victory of God and his people. These visions allow the recipients to reinterpret their difficult circumstances in light of God's ultimate plan and in turn calls them to specific changes in belief/behavior.	#7- Offer Hope

Apocalyptic Context	Apocalyptic visions are a subset of prophetic works and must be interpreted and applied in light of their literary context. Additionally, they occur in the literary context of the canon of Scripture and should be preached in light of their contribution to the whole.	#8- Connect the Contextual Dots
		#9- Preach the Gospel
		#10- Reveal the Eschatology
Apocalyptic Rhetoric	Apocalyptic visions are designed to accomplish specific rhetorical goals: capturing attention, transforming perspective, comforting the suffering, encouraging perseverance, fostering worship, or calling for repentance.	#11- Aim for a Similar Rhetorical Effect
		#12- Plan Worship Services with Purpose

Scripture Index

Genesis
- 3 — 200, 203
- 12:3 — 128

Deuteronomy
- 28 — 197
- 32:35 — 195

Psalm
- 1:1 — 51
- 2 — 193, 194, 197
- 2:9 — 201
- 19:11 — 70

Isaiah
- 1-5 — 115
- 5 — 115
- 6 — 115
- 6:1-13 — 115, 117
- 6:1-14 — 6, 15
- 7 — 115
- 7-12 — 115
- 25:6-12 — 196
- 49:7 — 125
- 50:6 — 125
- 52:13 — 125
- 53:4-11 — 125
- 63:1-3 — 193
- 66:7-9 — 200

Jeremiah
- 23:5 — 125
- 33:15 — 125

Ezekiel
- 1:1-2:5 — 27
- 1:1-3:15 — 6, 15, 17, 19, 20
- 2:6-3:15 — 27
- 8 — 38
- 8:1-4 — 23
- 8:5-18 — 23
- 8:1-11:25 — 6, 15, 33, 93, 102
- 9:1-11 — 23
- 9:4 — 54, 55
- 10:1-11:23 — 24
- 11:16-20 — 126
- 11:24-25 — 24
- 37:1-14 — 6, 30, 129, 146, 153, 160
- 37:9 — 129
- 37:14 — 129
- 40:1-48:35 — 6, 23, 133
- 47:8-12 — 94

Daniel
- 2 — 118, 120
- 2:31-45 — 117
- 2:44 — 118
- 7 — 67, 69, 74, 118, 125
- 7:1-27 — 150
- 7:1-28 — 117
- 7:3 — 69
- 7:4a — 68
- 7:7 — 68
- 7:9-10 — 35
- 7:9-13 — 93
- 7:13-14 — 35
- 7:18 — 94, 147
- 7:21-22 — 147
- 7:25 — 95
- 7:27 — 94, 147
- 7:1-12:13 — 6
- 8 — 39, 58, 67, 76, 82
- 8:1-14 — 81, 176
- 8:1-27 — 176
- 8:3 — 177
- 8:3-4 — 177
- 8:5 — 67, 177
- 8:6-7 — 177
- 8:8 — 177
- 8:9 — 177
- 8:10 — 69, 178, 179

8:11-12	178	4:10	154, 186
8:13	178	4:11-12	82
8:14	178	4:14	82
8:15	58	5:1-2	70
8:15-16	178	5:1-4	13, 22, 45, 109
8:15-27	81, 176	5:1-11	89
8:17	58, 178	5:4	148
8:17, 19	178	5:5-11	66, 75
8:17-26	14	5:34	126
8:21	179	6:1-8	93
8:23	179	6:12	186
8:24	179		
8:25	147, 179	Matthew	
8:27	180	12:30	197
9:20-27	17, 18, 138, 163	22:1-13	196
9:24	54	25:10	196
10:13	72	26:29	196
11:40	25		
12:1-4	147	John	
		20:19-22	160
Zechariah		20:22	129
1:1-6	119		
1:7-17	34, 119	Romans	
1:8-17	72	5:10	129
1:10	34		
1:7-6:15	6	2 Corinthians	
1:18-21	128	10:3-6	43, 205
2:1	59		
2:1-13	101	Ephesians	
2:5	35, 102, 146	6:10-20	43, 205
2:6	94		
2:13	56, 57	2 Timothy	
3	175	3:16	2
3:1-10	182	3:16-17	1
4	82	4:2	2
4:1-7	64		
4:1-14	154	Hebrews	
4:2, 10	85	10:10	186
4:2-6	70		
4:6	83	2 Peter	
4:6-9	70	1:21	113

Scripture Index

Revelation
1	62
1:1	120
1:3	165
1:4	85
1:9-20	15, 16, 25
1:12	85
1:18	51
1:20	85
1:9-22:20	6
2:18-19	191
2:23	191
3:1	81
3:4-5	193
3:18	193
4-5	147, 155
4:1-11	23
4:4	193
4:5	81, 85
4:11	53
5:2, 7	41
5:11-14	155
5:12	56
5-6	35
6:1-8	72
6:9-11	107
6:10	103, 195
6:11	193
6-7	193
7	131
7:9	193
7:9-17	131
7:13-14	193
7:14	131
8:13	57
9:1-11	63
10:3	54
10:9-10	70
11	38, 199
11:1-13	65
11:1-14	99
11:15	143
11-12	144
12	43, 64, 66, 71, 80, 81, 162
12:1-2	200
12:1-6	87
12:1-12	60
12:1-17	199
12:3	87
12:3-4	200
12:4	201
12:5	201
12:6, 14	76
12:7	202
12:9	66, 67, 81, 87
12:10-12	203
12:13-14	204
12:15-18	204
12:16	35
12-13	37
12-14	199
13	69
14	191
14:1-4	95
14:6-12	71
14:9-12	38
14:12	72
14:20	65
15:6	193
16	105
16:14	24
17:3-5	66
17:9-10	62
17:14	194
17:18	66
17-18	38, 95, 96, 120
18	103, 128
18:1-24	93
18:4	103
18:24	104

19	196
19:2	104
19:6-10	196
19:11-16	35, 191, 192, 193
19:11-21	190
19:17-21	195, 197
20	37, 136, 140, 191
20:1-6	86
20:1-10	136
20:11-15	104
20:15	104
21	74
21:1	69, 94
21:3	94, 101, 133
21:4	94
21:7	166
21:12, 14	74
22:1	166
22:20	195

www.ingramcontent.com/pod-product-compliance
Lightning Source LLC
Chambersburg PA
CBHW070134080526
44586CB00015B/1690

"Ryan Boys fills a gap, a rather large gap, in the preacher's tool box: the ability to preach apocalyptic texts. Preaching and teaching from apocalyptic texts such as Daniel, Zechariah, the Olivet Discourse, and Revelation is no easy task. I recommend this volume to pastors and teachers who are passionate about proclaiming the whole counsel of God."

—**Benjamin L. Gladd**, Professor of New Testament, Reformed Theological Seminary, Jackson, MS

"Preaching the whole counsel of God means not avoiding tough apocalyptic texts. For those venturing into this oft-unfamiliar territory, Dr. Boys offers guidance that is exegetically robust and homiletically nuanced, yet crystal clear. The book left me more eager to preach apocalyptic passages and more prepared to do so in an edifying way."

—**Eric W. Zeller, Ph.D.**, President and Professor of New Testament, Gulf Theological Seminary

"Ryan Boys has written the "go to" book for preaching the apocalyptic literature of the Bible. No other resource that I know of combines a high view of Scripture, a knowledge of the original languages, deep research of the apocalyptic genre, and an understanding of expository preaching. And this is a book pastors like me need. This book will equip readers to confidently and responsibly preach the apocalyptic literature of the Bible in ways that will build up our flocks."

—**Chris Brauns**, Senior Pastor of the Red Brick Church of Stillman Valley, Illinois, author of *Unpacking Forgiveness*